THE COLOUR THERAPY WORKBOOK

Theo Gimbel is the founder of the Hygeia College of Colour Therapy in the UK and has pioneered the use of colour therapy in hospitals throughout the world.

Hygeia Institute of colour

Brook House

Avening

Tetbury

GL00.

01453   832150.
(Stroud)

THE
COLOUR THERAPY
WORKBOOK

THEO GIMBEL

DCE, MIACT, NFSH, MLHRC, BRCP,
CertEd

ELEMENT
Shaftesbury, Dorset ● Rockport, Massachusetts
Brisbane, Queensland

© Theo Gimbel 1993

Published in Great Britain in 1993 by
Element Books Limited
Longmead, Shaftesbury, Dorset

Published in the USA in 1993 by
Element, Inc.
42 Broadway, Rockport, MA 01966

Published in Australia in 1993 by
Element Books Limited for
Jacaranda Wiley Limited
33 Park Road, Milton, Brisbane 4064

Cover illustration *Spiral Head in Window* by Ellen Schuster
courtesy of The Image Bank
Cover design by Max Fairbrother
Designed by Roger Lightfoot
Typeset by Poole Typesetting (Wessex) Ltd
Printed and bound in Great Britain

British Library Cataloguing in Publication
data available

Library of Congress Cataloging in Publication
data available

ISBN 1–85230–388–3

Contents

ACKNOWLEDGEMENTS

I would like to thank Pauline Wills, without whose help through months of discussion and conversations there would have been a great deal missing from these chapters. She also did the complete typing from my handwritten originals.

INTRODUCTION

Colour therapy harnesses the energies of light and the colours of the spectrum to help a wide variety of health problems and to allow us to harmonize with our natural rhythms and energies, and generally to become more balanced. It does this by locating and then correcting colour imbalances in the aura, the energy field surrounding the body.

All true therapies acknowledge that the five senses are each gateways to healing. The eyes which give us sight are a gateway to colour healing; the ears which give us hearing are a gateway for music therapy; the sense of touch lends itself to massage; the sense of smell to aromatherapy and the sense of taste to our diet. Remember, we are what we eat and our diet plays a very important part in the healing process.

To be aware and to acknowledge our senses is important because in colour therapy we treat a person as a whole that comprises body, mind and spirit. Each of these three aspects contains colour which becomes finer and more ethereal as it reaches into the spirit of man.

As humanity evolves, our awareness and consciousness changes. It is for this reason that the techniques used in colour therapy have also evolved and changed. Perhaps it is because of this evolutionary change that there are now many different schools of colour therapy, each teaching a slightly different technique but all ultimately reaching towards the same goal. The important factor is that each school should provide a good training, enabling students to become proficient and competent in their art.

This book will introduce you to the history and application of colour therapy, and in particular to the methods I have developed over the past forty years. To give you a taste of this, I would like to describe briefly a typical colour healing session.

A COLOUR HEALING SESSION

First the patient is made welcome. A 'Stage Report' record is compiled. This is a record of the patient's past illnesses, the treatment received, operations, drugs, etc. The patient's present problem is recorded and he or she is invited to say why they chose colour therapy as a method of treatment.

We emphasize to each new patient that colour therapy is *complementary to qualified medical treatment* and that our supportive aims must always follow their medical doctor's advice and suggestions.

A 'spine chart' is then compiled (see p. 48). This is a chart of the human spine which we ask the patient to sign on the back. Their signature acts as a witness because it contains their energy, and it is this energy which we are then able to pick up.

We then dowse out each individual vertebra using a dowsing technique described on p. 50. Where a reaction is felt in the finger, which can take the form of pain, heat, cold or a prickling sensation, the relevant vertebra on the spine chart is marked with a cross in the centre.

This chart is then interpreted for the patient and the appropriate colours for therapy are selected.

The patient puts on a white robe (to prevent colour distortion) and is seated comfortably in the therapy room. The selected colour plates (made of stained glass) are fitted into the Colour Therapy Instrument (see pp. 44–6).

The instrument is then started. During the 19¾ minute session relaxing music is played. The treatment colour, with its complementary colour, is beamed at the patient in a fixed cycle which is timed by an electronic timer. The patient may talk or sleep during the session.

After the session, the patient is asked how he or she feels. Do they feel the colours inside the body? Do they feel increased well-being or any side effects?

Finally, a series of seven colour therapy treatments is advised, one per week, to give the patient's body time to adjust and respond.

OBJECTIVITY AND INTUITION

Always, without exception, anyone who wishes to learn colour therapy must accept the challenge that in the final analysis it is up to him or her to learn objectivity; to let go of all preconceived ideas, hold no fanatical beliefs and to stand, at least when working on behalf of others, as a neutral person with an ear to listen and an eye to see rather than to spend most of the time talking and being inquisitive.

Maturity is not necessarily linked to age and intelligence, but to a true will to observe and have only the patient's interest at heart. This in itself will open up the practitioner to respond, often in quite surprising ways. They may suddenly know exactly the right thing to do for the patient and the correct way of applying it. This knowledge comes from the intuition and it is only by standing and listening that we will hear and know.

Chapter 1

What is Colour Therapy?

*. . . and darkness was upon the face of the deep. And the Spirit of God
moved upon the face of the waters.*
    And God said, Let there be light: and there was light.

Genesis, 1:2–3

Thus darkness and light began the sacred dance of creation and
out of their dance were born all the colours of the rainbow.

Each colour holds within itself its opposite complementary colour.
You can experience this for yourself by doing the following
exercise.

Exercise

Take a white sheet of paper, not smaller than one square foot.
In the middle of the paper place a clear-coloured six-inch
diameter square or circle or any other shape that you wish.
Look at this colour for about a quarter of a minute. Now turn
over the paper quickly and look at the blank side. You will
find, after a short while, that its complementary colour will
appear. It will be very bright, almost like a light. The quality
of this colour will be like the colours found in the aura or
electro-magnetic field which surrounds a stone, plant, animal
or human being.

COLOUR AND THE ELECTRO-MAGNETIC SPECTRUM

Colour is a part of the electro-magnetic spectrum. Long before colour appears as the visible part of this spectrum, we find cosmic frequencies which have such a fast vibrational frequency that they cannot be measured. These rays are in the realm of darkness. Light can be measured against darkness and has a speed of 180,000 miles per second. When this slows down, we reach the point where colour begins. This starts with ultra violet and continues with the colours of the spectrum. The slowing down of this spectrum after it goes beyond infra red brings us into sounds which are beyond human hearing. This occurs at about 22,000 cycles per second (c.p.s). Sound then disappears and becomes a very slow beat which can decompose architectural structures. Finally it will stand still at zero (0) and can be seen as static form (see Figure 1.1).

Apart from the cosmic rays, all of the invisible part of the electro-magnetic spectrum is used by science or medicine, sometimes resulting in harmful side effects. The visible part of the spectrum, namely the eight colours (see p. 4), each one with its own vibrational frequency, is thought to have no effect upon us as human beings. Through research which has been carried out by myself and others in this field, such as Max Lüscher, Faber Birren, and Roland Hunt, to name but a few, it has been shown that this is untrue. One simple example of this research is the effect that red and blue light have on blood pressure. It has been proven that red light raises blood pressure whereas blue light lowers it.

All living things, including the human race, have their own vibrational frequency. Each muscle, bone and organ of the human body vibrates to its own frequency and it is these frequencies which produce the electro-magnetic field which surrounds us. This is also known as the aura. This electro-magnetic field or aura contains all the colours of the spectrum and they are constantly changing in volume, shade and density according to our state of health or mood.

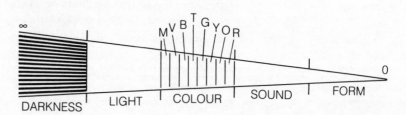

Figure 1.1 The Electro-Magnetic Spectrum

contains all the colours of the spectrum and they are constantly changing in volume, shade and density according to our state of health or mood.

According to Rudolf Steiner, Annie Besant and G.I. Gurdjieff, a human being comprises an ego, an astral, etheric and physical body. Steiner defines the ego as the consciousness and individuality of a person, which is linked to the higher or true spiritual self. It is from here that our true inspiration comes. The astral body (also known as the psyche or soul) is that part of us which feels emotion, harmony, and through which we experience peace and tranquillity.

.The etheric body houses the life force which feeds the physical body, keeping its energies in harmony and balance. It is these energies which can obey both our soul, and our ego. Indeed, if we think positively about ourselves it makes us feel better, allowing our soul to experience harmony. If we were able to live constantly in this state, dis-ease would be eradicated.

Through this teaching, Steiner creates for us a picture of man as a five-fold being:

- the spirit-self. God being (the part of creation where we would find the angelic world);
- the ego, personality, mental body which is already linked to our thought patterns;
- the astral, soul, feeling, emotional; that part of us where we can experience joy, happiness, fear, hate etc.;
- the etheric, life-force, metabolic; the area where energy is extracted from the food we eat;
- the physical body.

Further energies exist above the spiritual self and below the physical body, but these can only be experienced through the growth of consciousness.

All of these are represented in the electro-magnetic field or aura which surrounds us.

If any part of our being, any organ, muscle, gland or bone is out of harmony, then the frequency of its vibration changes and disease follows. This also brings about a change in the colours which surround us in our aura. What then is colour therapy?

Colour therapy is using the vibrational frequency of the colours of the spectrum to correct the imbalance or disharmony in the human body.

THE EIGHT MAJOR COLOURS

We can start at any time of the day or night to look at the colours which play around the earth as the sun circles this planet. Let us begin at the early morning hour when most of us are still asleep (see Figure 1.2).

It is 1 am and a very fine, deep colour emerges in this apparent darkness. It is the colour of purple. For the next two hours this royal colour prevails, changing imperceptibly towards violet as the hour of 3 am approaches. This is the night colour which surrounds us in sleep. Its very high vibration endows us with healing qualities needed in preparation for the coming day. Many children choose to be born at this hour because it is the hour of renewal. It is also the hour during which many souls choose to return to the world out of which they originally manifested. Time as we know it is measured by the earth's circulatory journey around the sun.

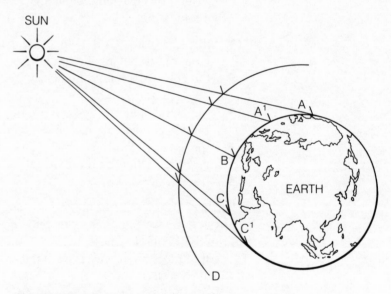

The light of the sun which comes down to the earth at dawn.
A   Very shallow and casts long shadows.
A¹   These shadows quite quickly become shorter.
At mid-day the shadows become very short.
The colours of the general atmosphere are coming out of the violet-blue gradually into the greens (B).
C   Early evening turns into the yellows, oranges.
C¹   The day ends with red before the sun sinks on the horizon.
D   This is the air cloak around this planet which makes the light visible.

Figure 1.2

Gradually the violet colour turns into blue as we approach the hour of dawn. This varies between 5 and 7 am, depending upon the time of year. The blue changes into turquoise and the freshness of this colour takes over the day. At 9 am this colour changes again into a peacock green spreading over the morning hours to 11 am, when a pure green emerges. This stays with us until the beginning of the afternoon. At 1 pm (13 hours) the atmosphere is filled with an apple green which has within it a hint of yellow. Towards 3 pm (15 hours) the true yellow begins which changes into orange at about 5 pm (17 hours). At this time people tend to relax. The worker goes home and joins his family or his companions. It is the hour to be social. The nineteenth hour (7.00 pm) has come and in the summer months the sun sinks as a beautiful red sphere toning the evening sky with red before night falls. This is the colour of strength and of life. Around 9.00 pm (21 hours), as the evening draws to a close, this red turns into a deep mauve. Night has started and as we sleep, the most beautiful colour of magenta takes us through the midnight hours from 11.00 pm (23 hours) to 1 am.

Some people may say that they can see these changes but most people cannot. To see them for yourself, take a photograph of a garden or landscape in the morning. Two hours later take another photograph of the same scene. Repeat this throughout the day. You will find that the result shows that each picture has a different colour overlaying the scene which you have taken. The photograph taken in the early morning will be much bluer and in the afternoon much yellower.

In the summer, go into the country, away from all the street lights and look up into the clear sky. You will see that the stars are set against a deep mauve − magenta − purple heaven. The colours are so deep that our eyes perceive them as black but I assure you that this is not so.

One thing should now have occurred to you and that is that the six night hours between 9 pm and 3 am display colours which are very closely linked in their hues, giving the impression that the colour changes are much slower. During the morning and evening the colour changes are quicker. This rhythmic movement can only be experienced as we become aware and try to observe it. This, of course, has an effect on those who work on night shifts out in the open.

When we take the colours which appear through the changes of the day and night and throughout the seasons of the year, we can see that each colour has an individuality and yet in spite of retaining this, it remains in harmony with the whole rainbow. In this wonderful sequence of colour, each colour has its own particular place.

By this phenomenon, we can know where a colour is when it shows itself. The orange stands between red and yellow. The green between yellow and turquoise. The blue between violet and turquoise and the red between magenta and orange.

Thus we have come in a full circle, or perhaps it is more correct to say that we have covered the first spiral, which has no beginning and no end. As it descends down the spiral, it goes into even stronger, darker colours and on the next ascending spiral into ever lighter shades.

Colour therapists begin to experience these perceptions as they become more aware of colour, its energy, its meaning and how it can be used to help mankind. The actual meaning of each colour will be explained in a later chapter.

Figure 1.3

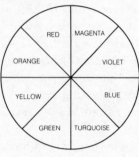

Chapter 2

A History of Colour Therapy

The old order changes, yielding place to new
And God fulfills himself in many ways
Lest one good custom should corrupt the world . . .
                    Alfred Lord Tennyson, *Morte D'Arthur*

Anthropologists have reported that prehistoric man was unable to see colour. This faculty developed later on in evolution and is still developing today. More people are now born with the ability to see the colours in the electro-magnetic field or aura which surrounds all living things.

ATLANTIS AND EGYPT

It is believed that in Atlantean times colour was used for healing. According to Frank Alpen in his book *Exploring Atlantis*, the Atlanteans built healing temples. These were circular in shape and around the circumference were individual healing rooms. When a person entered these rooms, they were enclosed by a crystal door. This was then energized to the frequency of the colour required. The ceiling of the main temple was domed and made of interlocking crystals. When the light shone through these crystals it formed patterns of colour and vibrations. Crystals and colour were used not only for physical ailments but also for the healing of relationships, and of emotional and mental imbalances. With colour they also used geometric forms, believing these to be as important as colour.

Archaeologists have discovered that Egyptian temples contained rooms which were constructed to allow the dissipation of the rays of the sun into the colours of the spectrum. They used coloured paints for their temple drawings and their hieroglyphics were equally beautiful in colour. These temples were used not only for worship but also for healing. It is believed that the sick were colour diagnosed and then put into one of the rooms surrounding the temple, which radiated the colour prescribed. This appears to follow closely colour healing methods of the Atlanteans.

The Egyptians also treated with solarized water. This is a method whereby water is infused with the vibrational frequency of a prescribed colour (by shining full spectrum light through a glass of spring water under a given colour) and then drunk in small doses over a set period of time — and it is a method still used today. The costumes worn by the people were made of natural colours. The priests' robes, however, were adorned with quantities of blue and gold. The knowledge of how dyes and bleaches were made were temple secrets. Writing, measuring, counting, weighing and how metals were correctly melted were only taught to the initiated priests.

COLOUR PIGMENTS USED IN ANCIENT EGYPT

1. *To be used on glass*

Dark blue	Cobalt
Light blue and green	Copper/green: iron
Yellow	Antimony and lead mixture
Rose-gold	Gold mixed with small quantity of iron
Red	Copper oxide

2. *To be used for painting (pigment colours)*

Except for black, all colours were of mineral origin.

Black	Soot with powdered charcoal Resin from trees as a fixing agent
White	Chalk or plaster (heated alabaster)

Red	Red ochre; iron oxide
Dark yellow	Yellow ochre derived from hydrated ferric oxide
Light yellow	Sesqui-sulphuret of arsenic covered with beeswax

Source: Gimbel, 1980, p. 52.

There is evidence from the Old Testament that people at that time were still clairvoyant. They were aware of and saw angelic beings and elementals. At times they appeared to be living in a dream state between two worlds.

In Egyptian mythology, the colours of blue, yellow and red were given to their various gods. They believed that blue rays were most powerful in the morning and in the spring and ascribed this colour to Thoth. Thoth was worshipped as a moon god and his name was sometimes given to the moon. Yellow was ascribed to Isis and thought to be the most powerful colour at noon and in the summer. Isis was the wife of Osiris and many things are attributed to her, including the civilization of Egypt. This came about through her teachings to women on how to grind corn, spin flax and weave cloth. She was also responsible for teaching men the art of curing disease. Red, believed to be strongest in the afternoon and autumn was attributed to Osiris. At first Osiris was worshipped as a nature god embodying the spirit of vegetation which dies with the harvest to be reborn again in the spring. Later on he was worshipped as god of the dead (*New Larousse Encyclopaedia of Mythology*, 1959).

The Egyptians, again like the Atlanteans, used gems in colour treatment. They proclaimed that gems are pure and contain concentrated colour, therefore having maximum effect upon the body. To treat with these, they ground up the stone and administered the powder to the patient. This follows the same principle as Ayurvedic medicine.

INDIA

From Egypt we come to India, a nation which has and still does use colour in its healing techniques, as can be seen in Ayurvedic medicine.

Indian philosophy sees man as a being who wears a coat of many colours. Colours which are continually changing according to his mental, emotional and physical well-being. This coat is composed of the seven bodies of man which interpenetrate each other and constitute the aura or electro-magnetic field which surrounds him. He is identified with the creative forces of the universe which are seen through the visible colours of the spectrum and the invisible colours not yet manifested upon earth.

The densest of the layers is the actual physical body containing the quintessence of all the aura layers:

Layer 1	The body
Layer 2	The etheric sheath
Layer 3	The astral sheath
Layer 4	The mental sheath
Layer 5	The higher mental sheath
Layer 6	The personality spirit
Layer 7	The higher self
Layer 8	The spirit self

Naturally, these layers become finer and finer, and after the eighth are commonly not visible, even to those who can see auras. There is a sense which picks up unnamed sheaths which reach into galactic space.

Contained within these bodies are the seven chakras or energy centres. These are likened to vortices of energy, each of which radiates one of the colours of the spectrum and is associated with one of the endocrine glands in the physical body. Indian physicians worked with these centres and the aura, looking upon them purely as energy which is either in or out of balance. If a person was ill, they looked not at the symptom of the ailment but treated them as a whole being which comprised body, mind and spirit. They looked for imbalances in the energy field and treated these imbalances with colour. This took the form of coloured gem stones or light. This, though not yet accepted by the medical profession, is the basis for colour healing today.

TRADITIONAL COLOURS AND UNIFORMS

Over the centuries, royal houses have adopted certain colours for their costumes and by these they have become known. The different colours of traditional dress adopted by different countries are well known and it is through these that we used to be able to identify where a person came from. The colours used in different parts of the globe were largely dependent upon the availability of certain minerals and their oxides. This tradition has almost been made extinct by the fashion world, in which certain colours are mandatory for certain seasons, disregarding the individuality and needs of each man and woman. In business men still wear grey and black striped suits, white shirts with white or blue collars because this is supposed to be businesslike. Even men who wear overalls for work are dressed in either green or blue. What people fail to realize is that the colour of the clothes we wear acts as a colour filter which is absorbed by our body. If we are able to become aware and tune into our body, we will know which colour we need to wear to create health and harmony in our whole being.

It is important to realize that colours used for clothes can be both a pigment colour and at the same time a colour filter. This fact plays a very important part in colour therapy and will be enlarged upon in a later chapter.

In earlier times, armies wore red uniforms with beautifully embroidered jackets, epaulets, sashes and stars. The buttons of the jacket were a gold colour. The higher the rank, the more elaborate the embroidery. The richer a monarch was, the more glorious his uniforms. This showed that he, the king, was a rich and powerful person. Today khaki and very earthy colours are used to act as a camouflage to deceive the enemy.

As well as blue and grey (the colours of regulation) business men dress and surround themselves with brown, the colour of commitment. They wear brown suits and sit in brown panelled offices with brown carpets. The monks and nuns of the order of St Francis wear brown habits, showing that they have committed themselves to their chosen profession and vows which they have taken.

Scottish tartans date back to the times when it was traditional for families to wear their own colours in the clothes which they wore, namely the kilt. The design and colour of the tartan worn identifies the clan to which they belong, i.e. the Campbells or the Stuarts.

In 1856 there was a major chemical discovery. Sir William Perkin made the first synthetic dyestuff through a distillation of coal-tar products. These were called aniline dyes and they revolutionized the dyeing industry. Mauve, which is reddish violet, was the first of the aniline dyes. Magenta, a red-purple, is another dye which was first prepared in the mid-nineteenth century.

There is no danger from aniline dyes once the dye has been

fixed. Only during the process, before the dye is fixed, is it poisonous. Although the advantage of dyeing with aniline is that the colours will not fade, unfortunately these colours are no longer so beautiful and alive. An experienced eye can easily detect the difference between these and natural colours.

COLOUR IN THE CHRISTIAN ERA: STAINED GLASS

In the fourth and fifth centuries, the start of the Byzantine era, art followed a set tradition in these early Christian times.

In the mosaics and the stained-glass windows of churches and cathedrals, blue represented the heavens and red the royal ruler, either the king or emperor. Maria (mother Mary) was represented as the Queen of Heaven. She wears a blue cloak and a red dress signifying her special task for this world which is carried out with love. The colours used for church windows up to the seventeenth century show that a clear pattern was followed, laid down from an older tradition in which the artist learnt from his master. At the end of the seventeenth century and beginning of the eighteenth century, a gradual change began. This started with paintings, followed by the colours used in church windows.

The colours in the stained-glass windows of Chartres Cathedral, exhibit a special kind of light. The same is true of the Stephans Kirche in Mainz. The stained glass used in such cathedrals or churches has been very carefully made by craftsmen, glass blowers and glass makers who knew that the full colours can only be achieved through very pure oxides such as gold, silver and copper. In 1947, Chagall, the great Jewish artist, was persuaded by a Christian priest to design and make the stained-glass windows for Stephans Kirche. He asked him to do it in order to make a new link between the Christian Germans and the Jews after the fall of Hitler. Chagall was a deeply religious man with a great depth of spiritual knowledge. He knew how to use colour to express spiritual depth through stained glass – and Hitler had fought all people who followed a spiritual path. This was the last of Chagall's work and he died before the windows were completed.

The windows in the Gœtheanum in Donach, Switzerland, were designed by Rudolf Steiner. This unique, vast building was built to hold a very comprehensive school of learning. The Gœtheanum is the centre for the study of all human arts, linking these to the divinity and spiritual path of mankind. Goethe began to see these

human potentials and Steiner built his further teachings upon
Goethe's. Each window is made out of one inch thick pure blue,
green, rose and red plate glass. Each plate is more than 2 sq.
metres, and four of these plates of glass are mounted on each
other, making a window of 8 m high, 2 m wide. The designs are
ground out of this glass so that the very thin colours which are left
are the light part of the designs. These windows affect a person
greatly because the designs and colours act as a medium for
meditation.

Sitting in front of these windows the colour is absorbed by the
person and induces a state of consciousness according to the
particular colour.

Blue	relaxation and peace
Green	balance and cleansing
Violet	dignity and self-respect
Rose	spiritual love

Many of the stained-glass windows which are designed today are
designed with a New Age consciousness, a state of mind which
has come about through the path of meditation, which has only
become generally known about since the end of the Second World
War.

J. W. Goethe in his work *Die Farben Lehre*, published in 1810 and
translated incorrectly as 'The Theory of Colour' instead of 'The
Teachings of Colour', shows how colours are the children of light
and darkness. J. M. W. Turner, the famous painter, used Goethe's
work extensively for his pictures.

Sir Isaac Newton (1642–1727) discovered that when daylight
entered the dark room in which he was working, the colours of the
spectrum appeared. From this discovery, he carried out a scientific
appraisal of colour. Sir Isaac Newton and Goethe complement
each other in their writing. They are both correct in their findings
which were arrived at by different approaches. Newton is very
scientific and factual in his observations whereas Goethe gives the
psychological, soul experience of colour.

More recent writers and explorers in colour therapy include
Babbitt, Ousley, Roland Hunt, Dinshah, Faber Birren, Proskauer
and Steiner. Steiner also writes about the use of colour in healing.
The Camphill schools, founded by Dr Karl König, and the colour
awareness techniques used in all the Rudolf Steiner schools are due
to Steiner's influence.

Professor Ronald Gregory of Bristol University was one of the first people to relate colour to psychology. I remember in the 1950s when I mentioned to educational psychologists the important part colour should play in their work, their reactions implied that this was nonsense and in no way were colour and psychology connected. Professor Max Lüscher has proved beyond doubt that colour and the psyche are linked and that colour can help the personality. He discovered that when people see a colour they have a particular personal reaction. However, he also found that there is a general objective reaction. His work on 'personality' was built on these discoveries, testing over many years both individuals and groups of people.

Out of these early explorations and findings has come what is today accepted as colour therapy.

In 1956, I started in a very primitive way to experiment with colour. Through this I realized that there is also a form element connected to colour. Blue, for instance, contained in a circle, has a different energy and meaning from when it is contained in a square or triangle. These findings also apply to the remaining colours of the spectrum. We will go into more detail on this in the next chapter.

Chapter 3

What Colour Can Do For You

'I am in the right place, at the right time, for the right purpose'
Anonymous

LIGHT AND COLOUR

Colour is a doorway, a starting point which leads deep into the mind and soul. It has the ability to affect all living things both consciously and unconsciously.

Light splits itself up into all the colours of the rainbow when it reaches the area between ultra-violet and infra-red on the electro-magnetic spectrum. When the frequencies of this spectrum slow down to ultra-violet, the human eye starts to perceive the first rays of magenta, often mistaken for pink. From magenta the other colours of violet, blue, turquoise, green, yellow, orange and red appear. After red, the rays again become invisible as they sink into infra-red.

The human body is light-sensitive, allowing colour to be absorbed through its cell structure as well as through the eyes. This means that blind people are equally receptive to colour.

THE FIVE SENSES AND THE ELEMENTS

Around all structures is a field of subtle energy which is invisible to the 'normal' senses. This is known as the aura. Our so called normal senses consist of:

sight which is connected to the element of fire;
sound which is connected to the element of air;
taste which is connected to the element of water; and
smell which is connected to the element of earth.

The fifth sense, touch, is connected to the etheric energy. It took many years of research before this energy was accepted as being vital to life. It surrounds all living matter and sensitive people can sense through their hands this energy around crystals, stones, plants and humans.

Everyone, unless blind, can see with their eyes the physical body but the etheric energy and aura are experienced through our higher senses. Steiner speaks of twelve senses – which leaves us with seven above the normal five. These seven we are able to develop as our awareness grows, enabling us to 'see' what to many remains unseen.

The auras around dense matter, such as minerals, portray very bright colours. The aura surrounding stones is mainly white with a very fine magenta tint. Plants have a golden aura, animals mainly blue and a human being has a multi-coloured aura. We will look at this in more detail in the next chapter. First, let us examine the energies which each colour transmits and some of the ways that they can be used in healing. Even though it is possible for people to treat themselves with colour, it is always more beneficial to attend a qualified practitioner.

THE COLOUR ENERGIES

RED	A beautiful clear mid red not leaning towards either orange or deep purple
Meaning	Strength, energy, vitality, life, sexuality, warning, power, alertness, contraction.
Therapeutic use	Low blood pressure, lack of energy, impotence, inactivity, drowsiness
ORANGE	A joyful, cheerful colour. Lifting out of the red towards yellow
Meaning	Happiness, dance, joy, independence, carelessness, uplifting
Therapeutic use	Antidepressant, energy also for low blood pressure when red is too powerful
YELLOW	The colour nearest to the light
Meaning	Detachment, intellect, thinking, judgemental, criticism
Therapeutic use	Rheumatism, arthritis, controlling calcium process

GREEN	The colour of nature and the plant kingdom
Meaning	Harmony, balance, stability and neutrality
Therapeutic use	Cleansing, purifying, cancer

TURQUOISE	A clear fresh morning colour
Meaning	Purity, immunity, calmness
Therapeutic use	Anti-inflammatory, AIDS (HIV), nervous tension

BLUE	The colour of the sky and sea, receding into the distance
Meaning	Relaxation, sleep, peace, expansion
Therapeutic use	High blood pressure, stress, asthma, migraine

VIOLET	An uplifting spiritual colour
Meaning	Dignity, divinity, honour, value, hope
Therapeutic use	Hopelessness, lack of self-respect, loss of self-appreciation, building personality.

MAGENTA	A colour of the highest order
Meaning	Selflessness, meditation, perfection, release, let go
Therapeutic use	Changes, freedom, to let go of old habits no longer applicable. The final transition into spirit at the correct time.

WHITE	The colour that contains all colours
Meaning	Innocence, untouched, isolation, wisdom, representing the priest
Therapeutic use	Total neutrality, absolute clarity and truth

BLACK	The unfathomable depth, holding all colours which are earthbound. Experience
Meaning	To attract, humility, negativity, knowledge personified, science.
Therapeutic use	Not applied in colour therapy

GREY	A colour which denies being a colour
Meaning	Service, dedication
Therapeutic use	Pride, haughtiness (rarely if ever used)

BROWN	The colour of the earth, death
Meaning	Sacrifice, dedication, commitment
Therapeutic use	Only applied in colour therapy to those who are completely selfish, not making any contribution to anything or anybody. In this case the colour should be worn in a dress or suit

COMPLEMENTARY COLOURS

Each of these colours has its complementary. Both the colour and its complementary are used in colour therapy (see p. 44). To find the complementary colour, look at Figure 3.1.

THE EYES AND COLOUR

Figure 3.1

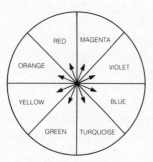

Colour is influential in the focusing of the eye. Blue focuses in front of the retina, red behind the retina and green on the retina. Blue light, which is also daylight, is the kindest light for the human eye.

Colours always work in complementary ways. This is also true of our eyes. When the rods and cones in the retina focus on one single colour, they will naturally produce the complementary colour. People are usually unaware of this because they do not allow time to experience this change. During this change, our eyes go into contraction and expansion, causing movement to the whole cell structure. As well as activating the rods and cones, we activate the muscles of the iris. This experience should keep the eyes healthy and strong. Why then are we faced today with so many eye problems which are diagnosed by the optician as normal deterioration?

About two hundred years ago, eye problems of today's magnitude were unknown. This is partly due to the fact that in our present age, more people read, write, drive and watch television. Another major factor is the arrival of VDUs (visual display units). Experts have said that the green screen of these display units would not change the focus of the eyes. This is not true: green destroys bio-chemical structures and therefore this colour cannot be beneficial to the eyes. Because green light breaks down all bio-chemical cells in their early stages, it can, however, be very helpful as a complementary therapy in healing cancer. Via the eyes, relayed to the pituitary gland, it directs the body and, under doctor's supervision, can be very successful. Pregnant women need to be careful, however, with VDUs.

All living things breathe, and so should the eyes. The research which I have carried out, using colour in order to keep the eyes alive, has resulted in the production of the Eye Strengthening Chart. This chart has been so effective over the past twelve years

Figure 3.2 The Eye
Strengthening Chart

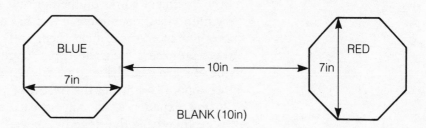

that people can now read and see small objects which, before using this chart, they could not do (see Figure 3.2).

The Eye Strengthening Chart should be stood up at eye level and used under good daylight conditions (near a window in bad weather or winter).

Let your eyes rest on the blue and 'soak in' this colour until a luminous area appears around the octagon shape and the colour of the shape itself begins to change. Then look at the white middle until a luminous, now glowing light appears. Let this fade and then rest your eyes on the red octagon again for a while until the same glow and change of colour appears around the red.

Return to the white centre and now see the whole glow appear again. Look for as long as it takes for this to fade out gradually. Then return to the blue and repeat this four to seven times, finishing up with the blue, not the red. Do this once or twice daily.

COLOUR AND HEALTH

Colour in the maintenance of health can no longer be brushed aside. Evidence has shown that it is a very significant factor in the improvement of patients' health. Doctors are now aware of the psychosomatic problems experienced by people. Not only is the physical body prone to suffer disease but also the soul (emotional area) and the mind. The mind affects the body, just as the body affects the mind.

Autism

Colour therapy can be a direct or indirect treatment, and therefore it is very suitable in helping autistic children. If possible, they should be treated as soon as the condition has been diagnosed.

The treatment works on the principle that because colour has a very high vibrational frequency, it has a very gentle effect upon such children. We can help them with this therapy but cannot always promise a complete cure. Fringe influences, such as their living environment, have to be taken into account, and these can either support or disrupt the treatment.

In my experience, all autistic children can speak. However, because they have developed at an early age a greatly increased level of consciousness, a high degree of shyness is caused. Even though they know how to talk, this shyness prevents them from doing so because they are frightened that they will make a mistake which would cause them a great deal of pain. Colour can be used to harmonize their extremely high perception levels and produce an extra invisible protective field around them.

Colour, like sound and radio waves, is an energy, but on a much higher frequency. It can therefore treat conditions which are caused by very fine imbalances in the body. It is completely safe and has no known side effects. Students studying colour soon realize how very integrated the spectrum is and learn to appreciate its beneficial effect upon the emotional and mental aspects of a person.

With autistic children, the treatment is known, by experience, to be a slow process, and regular treatment over a period of two to four years is necessary. With this treatment, patience has to be exercised while waiting for results. I feel that it is important to meet the parents with the child. At this meeting we discuss and explain how colour therapy works. The first consultation, which includes treatment, usually lasts for 1½ to 2 hours. This is then followed by monthly treatments.

VISUALIZATION

We could say that all dis-ease has a mental origin unless it is caused by an accident. Even then, the very first thoughts which follow that accident are important. Basically, there are two types of people. Those who lend their thoughts to negative, fearful images and those who rise above them and affirm that they will get better. These people can see beyond the momentary problem. Most powerful in all situations is an inner picture which ends with a solution to the problem (also known as visualization). The creative production of positive images is a vital training.

Nowadays this tends to be very weak because of the influence of television and films. Images arise out of a gradually developing memory. As we mature, we find that the images we make are richer and more complete. We can use these to help ourselves over many difficulties. The mind and the body must co-operate and we can use all images to increase our own health and well-being.

The making of images starts by relating words or phrases to a picture which is made up of past memories. Very often it also hinges on aromas. The sense of smell is a very powerful agent and should only be introduced into a therapy by a qualified therapist.

Children pick up positive and negative images very quickly. By the age of three, children love to hear stories which enable them to make their own images. Even the horrible witch and the nasty giant are only as bad and horrible as the child can make that creature out of past experiential memory.

The visual memory of children is enormous. Because they do not read or write they are much more observant and store in their minds what we adults look up in encyclopaedias. They quickly form images out of words, and from descriptions in tales and stories they make pictures in their minds, remember pictures and learn to 'dream visualize' their personal scenes. Television, however, takes away this creativity and damages this capacity. In all of my work since 1967, we have used this visualization process. It is a technique that goes back to Steiner who introduced it into meditation.

Relate images to your own needs, swim with the river and use its current as a means to approach the present stage in which you find yourself. Co-operate with the forces which surround you, even if at present you are unable to accept them all. Be awake, and at every turn in the river's course, look to see if there is something which you can use to help yourself. Those who swim against the river's flow can rarely win. In extreme situations, anchor the mind on to a meaningful familiar image, mantra, prayer or story. It will lead you out of the problems into a new stream of energy which perhaps you could not recognize before now.

What the inner self does, while the outer self complies with present circumstances, always leads to a new capacity. We can remain strong in our own inner being and do not have to conform as long as we do not offend or injure anyone or anything. When we say that something does not work, we have made a statement which must have a complementary reality, namely 'It does work.'

Visualization is a technique where we form positive images of colours and pictures which helps us to change the dis-harmony in our body to harmony.

Asthma

A complaint suffered by a lot of people is asthma. This can have many causes, but the symptoms are difficulty in breathing caused by spasms of the smooth muscles that lie in the walls of the smaller bronchi and bronchioles, causing the passage ways to partially close. A colour very conducive to easing an attack is blue light because blue light expands all biochemical structures. When using coloured lights as a therapy, it is important that they have dimmer switches so that they can gradually be turned on and off. If you are treating yourself with colour you should only wear white otherwise the colour of the clothes which you wear acts as a coloured filter and the colour which the body absorbs is a combination of the light and your clothes.

Asthma sufferers should not wear red or black. To reduce an attack successfully the person should wear white or blue. Red cloth, but even more powerfully, red light always contracts all biochemical cells exposed to it; blue cloth and blue light expand cells and are very helpful for asthma, migraine, stress, high blood pressure and general respiratory problems.

Some attacks are known to have an underlying rhythm. Some occur at night, others in the early morning or late afternoon. If you suffer from this complaint try and discern which pattern your attacks follow. Have a blue light available so that when an attack starts you can slowly switch this light on.

Breathing in colours

S.K., another of our patients, came complaining of sleeplessness. This had started after an accident two and a half years ago, in which she had sustained a knee injury. Since that time her knee had not been free from pain and she had difficulty in bending it. On examination, I noticed that it was very badly scarred and unusually warm to touch. This suggested that inflammation was still present.

I made a chart for her (see Chapter 5) and the diagnostic colour that it revealed was turquoise. I instructed her to breathe in turquoise and to breathe out red for at least five minutes each

Visualization for asthma and claustrophobia sufferers

It is a cloudy grey day and you are in a small boat on a canal. The banks have become quite steep and as you look ahead, a lock comes into view. On either side of the boat are very dark walls. As you drive or row into the lock, the sluice gates close behind you and for a moment you find yourself in a dark space. There is so little light and you feel that there is so little hope. You look up to the sky and the sky looks down upon you. The sound of rushing water meets your ears and the panic of being enclosed, shut in, is slightly eased. The feeling of hope unlocks a little of the anxiety. The boat is lifted up as the water rises and the hope of freedom grows. The dark walls of the lock become less visible as you rise to the new level of the canal. Just as the upper lock is beginning to open, the clouds part and the sun shines on to the new level of water to which you have risen. The upper lock gates are now fully open and your boat sails into the clear, free stretch of the canal. The green grass on either side of the canal allows you to change your feelings. You choose the feeling of freedom created by the open free space. This holds a promise for the future. The blue sky shines down on this scene. You have made it.

This visualization will gradually evoke a mental, emotional reaction as you visualize the last rays of light as you drive into the darkness of the lock. Therefore the whole picture becomes one event which is out of time and space. When you are next in a situation which has previously caused you problems, take the whole visualization into yourself and all the necessary images will immediately arise.

'Canal journey, boat, lock, darkness, clouds, rush of water, rising water level, sunshine, upper lock gates open, freedom ahead'.

This can finally be summed up as:

Darkness is followed by light.
Darkness equals light.
Light follows darkness.

In this way you have overcome the usual fear because you are able to be your own conductor, director of your health. Thoughts and emotions now control the metabolic and physical events so that your cell structure does not have to contract any more. It behaves in a healthy way.

The above story was written for Clifford S., a patient who suffered with asthma.

night before she went to sleep. When I saw her the following week, she reported that she had followed my instructions and had had four nights' uninterrupted sleep. She continued with this exercise on my instructions: her disturbed nights gradually diminishing and the swelling and pain in her knee subsided.

High and low blood pressure

Another complaint that can be alleviated with colour is high or low blood pressure. Blood pressure is the pressure exerted by blood on the wall of a blood vessel. Blood pressure is generated by cardiac output which is determined by the rate and force of the heartbeat and the resistance to the flow of blood through the vessels. An increase in the heart rate and an increase in resistance increases blood pressure. The reverse applies for low blood pressure.

If suffering from low blood pressure, the colour to use is red. Again this can be applied with the aid of a red bulb or through red clothing. Another way in which you can treat yourself is to obtain a full-length piece of cotton or silk dyed, with a natural dye, to the colour required. Lie under this in a bright sunny room, either dressed in white or, if it is in the privacy of your own home, naked, for twenty minutes each day. If you suffer from high blood pressure the same procedure applies, except that you would use blue instead of red.

Other disorders

Living in the twentieth century, with all its haste and problems, creates a lot of stress and tension. If this is not eradicated, it can lead to more serious problems such as cancer which can be helped with green light. Blue light is excellent against stress. Again you can use a blue bulb or a full-length piece of material.

If you suffer from insomnia, try sleeping in blue sheets, wearing either a blue or white nightdress or pyjamas. Have a blue light burning in the room. This form of treatment is much better than resorting to sleeping tablets. Sleeping tablets have side effects, colour does not.

Depression or lack of energy can be treated with orange. If you suffer from a skin complaint, try using yellow light on it. Yellow is also good for arthritis. If you have cut yourself and it has turned septic, try shining a turquoise light on it. If you have a sore throat, tie a turquoise scarf around it.

These are but a few of the ways in which people can help themselves with colour. If you have a more serious complaint and wish to be treated with colour therapy, do seek the advice of a professionally trained practitioner.

The golden ball

To conclude this part of the chapter, I would like to tell the story of how a little girl in Germany used colour to help herself.

Claudia came home from school very upset and in tears. When asked what the problem was she said that her classmate had got all the children to 'gang-up' on her. She wanted to be friends with her classmate but at this precise moment she hated her.

I told her that hate will only create more hate and that she must learn to love. That no one really hates or is nasty but that people can be got at by things which are making hate or making nastiness. I also told her that sometimes things happen to make us aware that nasty things also have the power to become nice. She listened and then asked me how she could make peace with her school friend.

I told her that she should go into a very quiet place and think of a golden ball and then ask her guardian angel to fill this golden ball with love. After she had done this she should put her friend and herself inside it so that they could both be surrounded by this love and forget the nasty things which had happened.

Claudia went to bed and made her special visualization. When she went to school the next day she had no fear. A few weeks later, I received a letter from Claudia. It read:

> Dear Theo,
> The golden ball worked wonderfully.
> I imagined my school friend and myself in a beautiful desert. We were enveloped by a golden ball in which was mirrored a rainbow.

> Yours Claudia

I had not said anything about a rainbow, but is this not a symbol of peace?

I learnt this method during my time as a prisoner of war in Russia. It works wonders. Children should be taught how to do this so that violence can be diminished. If schools were open to accept these teachings, I feel that we would be able to help those youngsters who are disturbed or violent.

THERAPEUTIC USE OF COLOUR IN ART AND DESIGN

How people experience colour in paintings, posters and everyday objects depends upon their state of well-being. A pretty landscape, yacht or beautifully painted flowers can make a good decorative setting under the so-called 'normal' state of mind. The same picture viewed by a patient in a hospital, surgery or clinic more often than not causes them to feel 'shut out' from it because it tries to give the impression that all is well when inwardly the patient or observer knows that with them all is not well. This then produces an introverted state of mind which can result in them not being able to communicate with the doctor whom they have come to see. It can save valuable time for both patient and doctor when the patient comes into the treatment room with an open and questioning mind.

It is therefore important that pictures, as well as decor, should be chosen to aid communication and treatment. Images which cannot be appraised in terms of depicting representational art are of enormous value in helping to restore mental, emotional and physical health.

Chapter 4

The Aura and the Chakras

If the light of a thousand suns suddenly arose in the sky, that splendour might be compared to the radiance of the Supreme Spirit.
And Arjuna saw in that radiance the whole universe in its variety, standing in a vast unity, in the body of God . . .

(Bhagavad Gita, Ch. 2, v. 12–13; translated by Juan Mas Caro, Penguin Classics)

AURAS

All things that are visible, from stones to plants, animals, human beings, water, fire, air and minerals contain energy. Generally we are able to weigh, measure or quantify this energy by one method or another.

For many people, this knowledge is sufficient. However, as we move towards the twenty-first century, more people are beginning to sense that all objects which are visible also have an invisible counterpart. This invisible energy can be likened to a magnet. Only a few see the force which surrounds a magnet, known as magnetism, but its existence can be proven by showing its power to attract metal objects to it.

In the same way, around all things visible is an invisible 'cloak'. This is known as the aura or electro-magnetic field. The auras around dense matter, such as minerals, portray very bright colours. The aura surrounding stones is mainly white, with a very fine magenta tint. Plants have a golden aura, animals mainly blue and a human being has a multi-coloured aura.

The aura of a human being is egg-shaped. It extends approximately 36ins above the head, gradually diminishing in size until it closes under the soles of the feet. Inside this is a smaller cloak which extends about 4ins from the physical body and which is known as the life-force field or etheric sheath (see Figure 4.4 p. 31).

Everyone, unless blind, can see the physical body with their eyes, but the etheric energy and the aura are experienced through our higher senses. Rudolf Steiner speaks of twelve senses which leaves us seven above the normal five. These seven we are able to develop as our awareness grows, enabling us to 'see' what to many remains unseen.

The human aura comprises many layers, each radiating its own ethereal colour. The layer nearest to the physical body is known, as already mentioned, as the etheric sheath and it is this which houses the energy channels (nadis) which absorb prana or life force from the atmosphere, and the energy centres or chakras. There are seven main chakras situated at the border of the etheric body and known as lesser chakras. Each of these has its complementary chakra, known as the greater chakra, situated at the border of the aura. Very few of the people who have the gift to see auras can actually see the greater chakras.

THE CHAKRAS

The chakras of human beings are, in an amazing way, made up of a complete rainbow. Basically, they are like lenses of a telescope. These lenses collect energies or life force which is then conducted to the endocrine glands of the physical body which they serve. A single chakra, seen within the aura, never stands still. It follows a general pattern which can be strong and filled with life energy. It can also be temporarily weak. This usually shows in the brilliance or weakness of the colours. In Figure 4.1. A indicates where the greater chakra is 'seen' or rather perceived, and B how it passes through the lesser chakra.

Both the greater and the lesser chakras collect from the energy field (the aura). This is needed in order to maintain the life of the endocrine glands which they serve. They are like selective filters which select by way of colour.

Figure 4.1

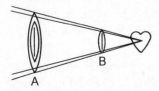

The lesser chakras, situated in the etheric body, resemble a line of rotating discs which form a column of luminous light. Each one contains all the colours of the spectrum but displays one dominant colour. The first or base chakra displays red; the second or sacral chakra orange; the third or solar plexus chakra yellow; the fourth or heart chakra green; the fifth or throat chakra blue; the sixth or brow chakra indigo; and the seventh or crown chakra violet. Above these seven main chakras are three higher chakras which radiate magenta, white and the sacred darkness out of which all things become manifest.

THE COLOUR ORDER OF THE CHAKRAS

Knowing that each of the chakras, lesser and greater, contain all of the colours, let us take the heart chakra, as an example, to see how the colours are arranged.

In the heart chakra, it is the colour of green which causes balance, cleansing, equilibrium and life renewal. Thus, the outermost layer of this chakra is green. In the order of the colour spectrum, the next colour layer will be turquoise, then blue, violet, magenta, red, orange and yellow at its centre (see Figure 4.2). This is the greater chakra order. The lesser chakra reverses this order showing yellow on the outside and green in the centre (Figure 4.3). This system follows through each of the individual chakras in order to give life and vitality to each of the endocrine glands.

As the order of the colours of these two chakra systems are complementary to each other, we can see that nature responds to the constant needs of the wholeness of man who is working with these two forces. Like a question and answer, this is the principle by which we find the instructions for our journey. In this balance

Figure 4.2

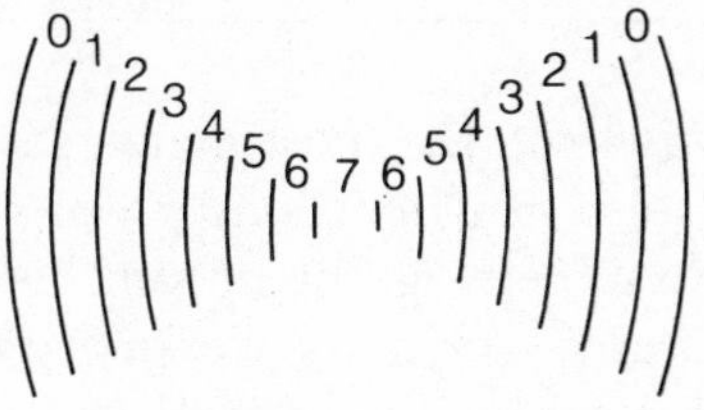

Figure 4.3

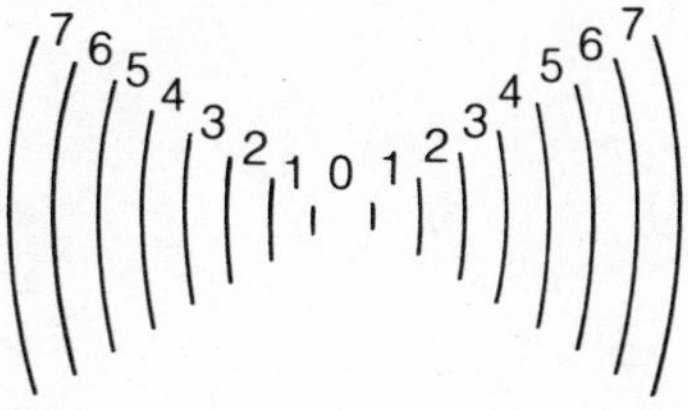

0 = the colour which represents the main colour of the aura, the remainder are as follows:

0 = the heart chakra = green

1 = yellow ☐   2 = orange ☐   3 = red ☐   4 = magenta ☐

5 = violet ☐   6 = blue   ☐   7 = turquoise

of the colours, we find in the middle of each chakra, violet and magenta (Figure 4.2). Violet denotes self-respect and dignity, and magenta denotes change and a letting go. These two colours work towards the spiritual energies which create the 'sacred heart', which thereby gives a renewal rhythm to the bloodstream. The heart is usually seen and understood to be the organ of love. The Christian Church connects the love of Jesus Christ to the heart and lifts this love into a more elevated love — without the slightest sexual implications — and which is the Sacred Heart. This has no passion, only love for all living beings. When we treat with colour, we take into account this renewal rhythm and use colour with its complementary. If this is not done, the bodily responses of a person respond negatively because the treatment is incomplete.

> As a practical exercise, take the other six chakras and work out their colour sequence. Discover the patterns associated with the greater and the lesser chakras. If you wish, you can then take a compass and draw eight ever-increasing circles on two separate sheets of paper and instead of putting numbers in the circles as illustrated in Figures 4.2 and 4.3, colour them with the appropriate colour. Replace 0 (zero) with 7 and zero will then come into the place of 1 (one). There will then be eight progressive pictures which will leave the spectrum intact but shift the colours so that red (base chakra) next time round becomes orange (adrenals), then yellow (solar plexus). This will give you drawings of all the chakras in turn as the outside colours are then showing that a full spectrum colour is the living colour of life.

In counselling, the most gentle suggestions are always far more acceptable than directions given with the implication that one must do something. By the same token, the more rarefied a colour, the better it works. By working with this principle, we offer the correct memory to the cell structure. Herbs and homoeopathic medicines are very successful because they follow this principle of gentleness. The pre-manifested forces, which to most people are invisible, are the aura and the etheric sheaths surrounding the visible kingdoms of the minerals, plants, animals and humans. These forces are so fine that they still respond to thought patterns, emotions and general modes of movements. We can with good guidance from a professionally trained colour healer, learn how to conduct these forces to benefit health. The regular practice of certain colour visualizations is very successful. They rely precisely on immeasurably fine chemical etheric changes which alter the often neglected behaviour patterns of our own views of health status. It becomes more and more obvious that the well-trained healer becomes the teacher of the patient, and by this method the patient conducts his/her own life forces using colours and experiencing the fine changes which occur through coloured lights.

AURA PATTERNS

The aura of a human being, as well as radiating all the colours of the spectrum, contains energy patterns. These patterns can change with diet, health, mood, emotional stability, etc. When a person is in good health, the chakras and energy patterns are in balance and the colours radiating in the aura are in harmony. In the following diagrams we start with the simple basic pattern of the aura.

Figure 4.4 The Approximate Size of the Human Aura
A: Longest Egg Shape
B: Etheric Sheath
C: The Physical Body

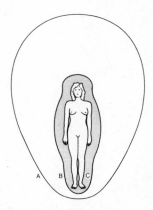

Figure 4.4 shows the basic three areas with the physical body in the centre. The physical body has been able to manifest through the energies of the aura and the etheric sheath, both of which were present before the physical body came into being.

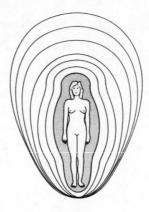

Figure 4.5 The Aura with the Horizontal Layers

In all living things, there lies a beautiful principle behind all growth. Each year a tree puts around itself two rings of new life. One fast, short one in the summer and one slow, hard one in the winter. Likewise an onion comprises many skins. As illustrated in Figure 4.5 the 'invisible' structure of the aura comprises 'horizontal' layers.

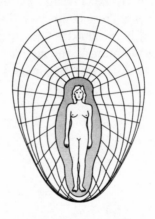

Figure 4.6 The Aura with Horizontal and the Vertical Layers

Where there are orbs or balls of energy, there is also a radiation pattern as indicated in Figure 4.6. Please try to see this not in two but three-dimensional space.

Figure 4.7 The Aura Showing the Halo and Wings

Potentially we are all endowed with the most wonderful patterns. When we can perceive these amazing designs we see within them wings and halos as in Figure 4.7. More and more becomes visible to us if we ask questions, and when we are able to ask clear questions, the answers are forthcoming.

Figure 4.8 The Aura with Wings and Extra Chakras, Anchoring Man into the Four Directions of Space

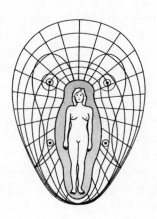

Figure 4.9 The Aura with the Column of Chakras In some teachings, taken from the Kabbalah, there are 18 chakras, but the ascending ninth chakra is overlapping here with the descending ninth chakra making a total of 17

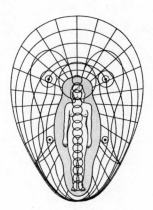

The number four is one of the most powerful numbers to anchor, to orientate and to secure mental, emotional, metabolic and physical structure, and the human body is no exception to this. Thus we have four main chakras built into the aura as in Figure 4.8. Two of these are acknowledged in the great gesture of blessing, given by a priest, when the palms of the hands are raised to bless his/her congregation. In the palms of the hands are also minor chakras and by allowing these to become channels of transmission, we are indeed using them to let the spiritual energies flow through.

In front of this wonderful 'Cathedral', our body (together with the aura, etheric sheath and all the beautiful structures within it), stands the bell tower, the church spire. In the case of the human person, this is the column of the chakras and it allows us to be conscious beings, standing upright, in proud humility, as my very dear teacher Father Andrew Glazewski would say.

GENERAL CHALLENGING PATTERNS

Frequently, there can be found in the aura distortions or discords. Long before any physical disease appears, we can detect in the aura certain symptoms that precede an illness.

Before we refer to this as 'illness', we should remember that what we identify as a poison to the physical body can also be a remedy. In the ancient temples, alcohol and smoke were used to bring about certain states of mind and emotions. This was achieved via the metabolic system which, with the intake of alcohol or smoke, or certain herbs, changes the personality of those being subjected to it.

In ancient times, the general pattern was not to dominate or dictate or to use politics, but a genuine, carefully conducted education or even initiation by those priests, who, incidentally, were also the doctors of the day.

We are now living in a vastly matured and very sophisticated world where a great deal of mistrust has developed and where people have free access to drugs, cigarettes and alcohol.

Figure 4.10 The Aura After Smoking or Drinking It can be cleared after 24 hours unless the person is a chain smoker or alcoholic

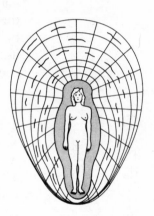

Figure 4.10 shows how fine clouds of mist-type flecks develop when a person smokes cigarettes and drinks alcohol. An occasional cigarette or glass of wine or spirits can be cleared out of the aura within 24 hours. These cloudlike flecks lie horizontally and can more easily be removed by the vertical, radiating aura energy.

You may call the effect of Figure 4.11 a sort of pollution. This occurs through the use of hard drugs such as LSD or heroin. These drugs cause a type of damage to the aura that cannot be so easily eliminated because the pollution is not a horizontally lying cloud, which is comparatively easily dispersed or cleaned out, but is like wedges or spears which cause cracks in the aura. Once these wedges have broken the aura there is no known remedy or cure.

Figure 4.11 The Aura Showing the Effect of Hard Drugs such as Heroin

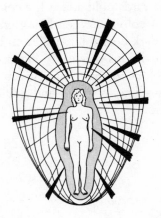

We will now look at some of the patterns in the aura which are connected with the soul and mental aspect of a person. There are energies flowing in and out of the aura which we can and should accept because they are healing and revitalizing. When they are in harmony with the need of a person, they do not create a 'visible' mark in the aura. However, there are situations when on one level, even a subconscious level, a person does not accept the energies, thereby causing a stoppage in their natural flow.

Figure 4.12 The Aura Showing the Effect of Energies Not Accepted by the Thoughts, Emotions or Metabolic System
These gradually weaken the health structure and produce the colour grey, with the effect that the person often tends to opt out of life

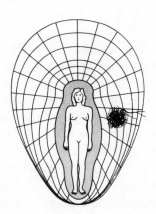

In Figure 4.12, instead of a fine clear colour on each level of the aura we see what looks like a knotted ball of grey wool. This is blocking off the unaccepted energies. Grey is the colour of fear and untruth and can accumulate in the aura. However, it serves all the colours of the spectrum and creates space in which there is freedom to change. It can accept light (white) and darkness (black) and has a leaning towards silver.

When the opposite to Figure 4.12 happens, a person is unable to let old, no longer needed, negative energies flow out of the aura. This also blocks up the aura (Figure 4.13). It happens mainly to people who cannot give freely, who accrue wealth and hold on to possessions which they do not need. These people have a lot of brown in their aura. Brown is the colour of commitment. In the last resort it is the colour of death in the physical state. Brown has a leaning towards gold and is the colour which in a way dominates over other colours. When living energy decays into the earth, it becomes dark brown humus. From this state new life can spring.

The conditions shown by Figures 4.12 and 4.13 respond very well to colour therapy when given by a qualified therapist. With this, counselling is given and advice on how patients can help themselves.

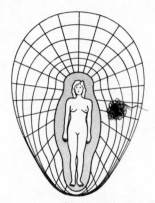

*Figure 4.13 The Aura Showing the Effect of Energies Not Released from the Body
These will stay in the aura, causing problems later*

There are many schools of thought on the chakras and each one in its own frame of reference has a part to play. The basic principle remains that there are energy patterns preceding any manifestation of living structures in all kingdoms of nature. As the human being becomes more and more aware, there appear more and more valuable insights, such as the number and the details of the aura and chakras.

When I first started to perceive the aura, I saw just simple outlines and very little else. As I researched more deeply, more details appeared. These always followed the original principle and laws of these phenomena. Figure 4.14 is based on two views which I have put together. The first is based on the teaching of the Kabalah and the second is based on sacred geometry. The result of using both of these teachings is that we find a column of eighteen chakras. Nine from the crown (the top of the head) down to the base chakra and nine rising from the soles of the feet to the base chakra, thus creating a wonderful mirror image. However, the rising column covers the descending one at the base chakra, the sacred centre, where two human beings can become 'one flesh'. Those people who practise reflexology (zone therapy) will now see that the washing of feet by a master is not just an outward ceremony but that a healing action is being performed. (See *John* 13:5, 'The washing of the feet by Christ'.)

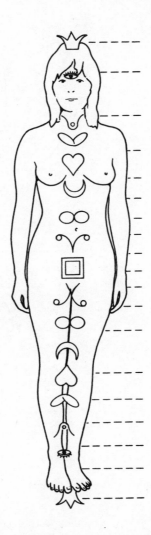

*Figure 4.14 The Scanning
Chart*

Figure 4.15 shows the image to which a therapist who can 'see',
that is perceive auras, will sooner or later come. This image shows
how a stage of enlightenment can be found. There are no quick
ways to learn to perceive the aura or, for that matter, to become
aware of the finer energy field around all manifested matter.
Stones, plants, animals and humans all have an energy field; what
needs to be learnt is how to make such 'vision' accessible. Through
training and guided advice, under the supervision and in the
presence of a conscientious teacher the double vibratory vision
can gradually develop. Double vibratory vision capacity, which
produces the aura picture either as a whole or in part, can happen
suddenly when the person is unprepared, in which case a person

Figure 4.15 The Raising of
the Centres

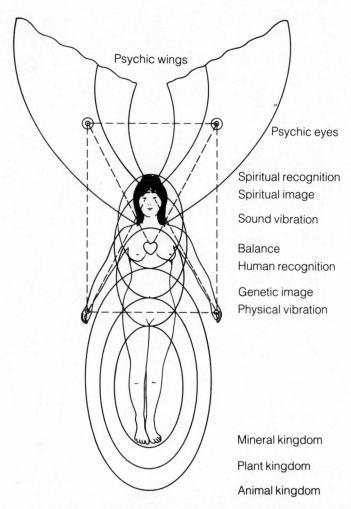

Psychic wings

Psychic eyes

Spiritual recognition
Spiritual image

Sound vibration

Balance
Human recognition

Genetic image
Physical vibration

Mineral kingdom

Plant kingdom

Animal kingdom

Source: Out of the exchange of experience with Dr Andrew Glazewski and the author, 1963–73

quite unexpectedly finds her/himself momentarily or for longer periods with this vision capacity. There are very fine means to help control such double vibratory vision: art therapy and good counselling. ECT, which causes the 'shut down' effect of such capacity, should be avoided and only be used as a last resort, if at all. This double vibratory vision can be learnt but only with great care and is in no way trial and error method. Personal dedication and very sound guidance are the only sure approaches, and I must emphasize this.

Each of the seven chakras which are involved here are using the centre, the heart, to lift the more physical energies into the more spiritual energies. Through this, a unification is established which brings the human being into contact with both the kingdoms below us, the elemental world, and the kingdoms above us, the angels. The colours which can be experienced range from very deep reds to very fine, almost invisible magentas.

THE TWO COMPLEMENTARY RAINBOWS

By now it should be clear to you that all things have their opposite or complementary image. Colour is no exception to this rule. Nature, like a human being, also reflects the innate phenomena of complementary energies. When we see a rainbow in the sky, there is always its complementary rainbow, though sometimes this is not visible to the human eye. The first rainbow mirrors and creates a second rainbow with its colours reversed. See Figure 4.16.

Through this we can personally experience that the spectrum is a circle of colour. The next time that you see a rainbow, be very observant and look at the colours. If you see a second rainbow, take the trouble to compare the two. The first rainbow will have green at its centre and the second will have magenta at its centre.

The second rainbow always appears above the first. Here the magenta colour outshines the green which lies behind it. In the

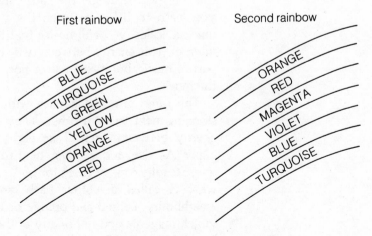

Figure 4.16 The Two Complementary Rainbows

The Two Complementary Rainbows

first rainbow, the green outshines the magenta. Because all of this is light, we cannot see through it. Also, coloured light cannot create colours such as grey and brown. These can only be created with pigment colours.

Here we are entering an area which is the bridge or transition between the manifested solid world and the pre-manifested invisible world. Just as these beautiful colours can only appear for a comparatively short time, so all living energy is in the process of letting go of the past, moving into the present and on into the future. So, when we see the rainbow appear, we come from the past, into the present and we wonder at the phenomena. It then disappears and is only left in our memory.

From the past, we can gather experiences which allow us to anticipate some future. When we gather the actual principles which stand behind all growth and all evolution, we can begin to see into the future. Variations and individual differences always signify that there is a law behind all living and loving events. When two energies meet at an equally measured strength and they are complementary, we can say that they create between them the third energy. It can be said that one and one make three and not two.

Take this same concept into music and we can start to hear that between an interval of two sounds lies the third energy. Sing an interval of a third or fifth twice. The first time sing it without a pause. The second time sing the same interval with a pause between the two notes. You will sense a tension. This tension we call energy. The longer the pause, the more you feel the energy. If you learn to listen between the various intervals contained in musical scales, you will notice that the energy changes with each interval. This energy between two sounds is actually the inaudible part of music, but, believe it or not, it is the actual healing part of the music.

The same principal applies with two colours when they are standing next to each other. They start to oscillate, creating an energy between them. Take eight pieces of different coloured paper (A4 size) and lay them next to each other without leaving a gap. Steadily look at them for up to 15 seconds. You will see that what is called a 'colour flash' arises. When the colours are 'neighbours', i.e. red and orange or green and turquoise, blue and violet, magenta and red or any of the mixtures which are possible between the eight colours, the energies are gentle. When, however, you use orange and violet or red and green, turquoise

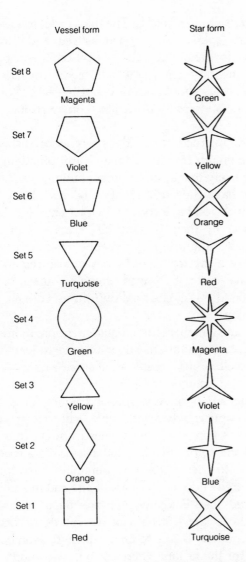

Notes on complementary energy

Human consciousness arises out of the swing between extremes, light–dark, hot–cold etc. This polarity principle is built into all things which we encounter. Thus vessel form (the feminine) has also the star form (the masculine) within. Neither have a purpose unless they actually relate to each other. Complementary forms are supported by complementary colours and sound is no exception. Both sound and the listening have to co-operate, sound being the masculine and the listening the feminine aspect. Explore further and find yourself standing right between these forces of polarity,. constantly struggling to keep the balance.

Figure 4.17 Vessel Form and Star Form   The energy of form is again a double energy and goes back to the ancient (sacred) geometry.

The vessel form (container) is linked to feminine energy, and the complementary starform is aligned to male energy. The syllable of 'gon' denotes the vessel and the 'gram' the star such as hexagon and hexagram (see Critchlow, 1969). Each aperture changes the grid of light and thereby conducts the colour each time in a new way. Basically all 'windows' are apertures and, according to their shape, change the light grid and create a certain atmosphere inside a room.

and yellow, you find certain discords. The third order possible is to use complementary colours only, such as red and turquoise, orange and blue, yellow and violet etc. With these there appears a wonderful complementary energy which seems to satisfy the sense of sight and brings about harmony, not tension. Work with these eight colours and find out which combination is most enjoyable for you.

Now look at the instructions on the energies of each colour. These you will find on pp. 16–17. You may learn something about yourself. It is most likely that at this moment in time, you need the colours which you have chosen to satisfy a need within yourself. Say, for instance, that you have chosen a violet and blue. Look at the meanings and apply them to yourself. Are you currently in need of self-respect and dignity? Has someone or something taken this valuable energy away from you? Do you also require peace and relaxation? Have you not allowed time for yourself but have been running around in circles? Allow these colours to be visualized within you.

Try to work out whether this requirement is momentary, temporary or for a longer duration. You may come to feel that you need violet and yellow to create a balance within you, or, alternatively, blue and orange.

Blue and orange are two very special colours for a human person. These two appear when you have achieved in yourself peace (blue) and joy (orange). If this applies through your whole being, body, mind and spirit, then you have achieved a wonderful harmony. Through experience, these colours have been found to be linked with children under eight years of age and in adults who are natural healers. Just imagine you are filled with peace, relaxation, joy and happiness. What else do you need? The most relaxed, joyful person who is able to be free from tension becomes a pure instrument for the healing energies to flow through them.

Chapter 5

RHYTHMS IN COLOUR

MEPHISTOPHELES: *Since thou O Lord again approaches*
Asking how all is shaping up down here
And thou art by and large well pleased
    to see me.
Thus I am also part of this assembly . . .
                    J. M. v. Goethe, PROLOGUE IN HEAVEN, FAUST 1

All life, including human beings and our planet, needs a challenge. This is the reason why we need the complementary energies which are inherent in all living beings.

Life depends upon the very fine balance of the colours and their complementary colours. It is when the balance of health is upset that colour therapy is given to restore harmony in the body. This is made possible because our bio-chemical structure is light-sensitive.

The very first colour-therapy instrument made by myself was programmed to administer two minutes of the colour needed by a person, interlaced with two minutes of its complementary colour (five on the increasing scale, four on the decreasing scale). This made nine changes, each change being of two minutes duration. However, when I discovered this was not working, I used a skin galvanizer and a blood pressure gauge, which gave no response after the third change on the colour-therapy instrument. This showed that the human body reacts very quickly to mechanical rhythms and 'switches off' when there is no more to be learnt.

THE FIBONACCI SERIES OF PROPORTIONS

While I was designing what came to be known as our Colour Space Illuminator, I was thinking about proportions. These should always be observed in design and I based the design of this lamp on the proportions of the Golden Mean. These rhythmic proportions were discovered by Fibonacci (qv), an eleventh-century monk who lived in Pisa, Italy. His original series of numbers were:

$$1 + 1 = 2$$
$$1 + 2 = 3$$
$$2 + 3 = 5$$
$$3 + 5 = 8$$
$$5 + 8 = 13$$
$$8 + 13 = 21$$
$$13 + 21 = 34 \text{ etc.}$$

These proportions are found in crystals, plants, animals and humans (see Figure 5.1). I felt that integrating them into the design of the Colour Space Illuminator made it into something very special.

Suddenly I realized that time and space are interchangeable. If this was so, why not use the Golden Mean proportions and transfer them into time for use with the colour therapy instrument? I worked with this idea and came up with a time-change sequence which was aligned to the vibrational harmony of the human body. I also realized that this sequence is deeply embedded in all nature. The sequence is as follows:

The instrument begins with a short 45 second exposure of the therapy colour and is followed with a 3¼ minute exposure of the complementary colour. With each change, the therapy colour increases from 45 secs to 1¼ mins, 2 mins, 3¼ mins, ending with a 5¼ minute exposure.

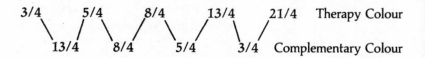

This totals 12½ minutes. In between each of these five exposures, the complementary colour appears in a diminishing order. It goes from 3¼ minutes down to 2 minutes to 1¼ minutes and ends with

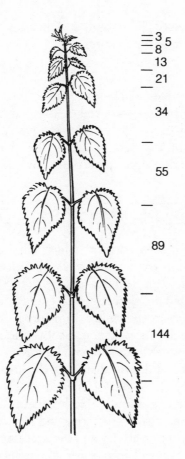

Figure 5.1 *The Common
Stinging Nettle
This displays very clearly
the rhythms in space which
we now use for time*

=3
=8 5
– 13
– 21

34

–

55

–

89 ·

–

144

–

Figure 5.2 *The Colour
Therapy Instrument*

Figure 5.3 *Graph of the
Rhythms of the Instrument*

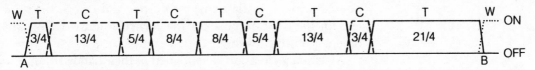

Explanation and key
The indicated fractions are $\frac{1}{4}$ of a minute. The following letters are:

W – Working light switched on manually.
A – Start of treatment operated by the therapist.
T – Treatment colour time on the increase.
C – Complementary colour time on the decrease.
The crossing over indicates fade-in and fade-out (2 secs).

At the end of the treatment ($19\frac{3}{4}$ mins) the working light will come on
automatically to signify the actual finish of the treatment. We have indicated
to the patient before the therapy has started that there is no rush
to get up after the treatment has ended.

a ¾ minute. This totals 7¼ minutes, making the complete treatment time 19¾ minutes.

$$12.5 \div 7.25 = 1.724.$$

This is a total Golden Mean rhythm.

The rhythm produced by these time changes presents a surprise element to the body which motivates the cell structure to expand and contract. Because all of the changes have a different time interval, the rhythm becomes alive and not mathematical.

HOW TO MAKE A CHART TO DETERMINE THE COLOUR FOR THERAPY

The central energy on which all things are based manifests in orbital form and linear rays of light issuing from the centre to the periphery three-dimensionally. In crystal growth it is multi-dimensional but in a geode this energy frequently streams from the periphery to the centre. In plants it is more orientated towards a vertical direction. In animals it is horizontal (based on the position of the spine). In the human during wakefulness and daily work it is vertical and during sleep, like the animals, horizontal. The spine is our central column of energy which is linked to the brain. Each vertebra has an outlet to the organs in the chest and trunk of the body, and also to the arms and legs. The spinal cord supplies the body with sensitivity and the necessary functions for our daily life.

The human capacity for communication is extremely complex. It can be by looking at another person, by shaking hands, kissing or embracing. If the last two are deepened it can, at the right time and for the right purpose for the particular individual, lead to the holy act of love making.

A person's vibration is contained in their handwriting, a lock of their hair, a drop of their blood or a photograph of them. In times past and even today, there is a ritual for a couple to exchange a lock of hair in order to be in touch with each other. If you travel away from home and are inclined to become homesick, it can help if you carry in a pouch a small piece of earth from your own garden.

In all of the above-mentioned things are contained energies which can be used by trained people in helping to harmonize and treat people, animals or plants which are sick.

When you write a letter by hand, you put part of yourself into it and this remains for a long time. When some of the natives of

Africa or America, for example, refuse to be photographed, it is because they have a deep inner feeling that something is being taken away from them. In a sense this is correct, but if we have their consent, then it is permissible.

The ancient art of using these very fine energies to heal or to communicate is known as dowsing. With this art we can establish a communication between ourselves and our patient. This can give us very accurate information about a patient, provided that we are able to exercise complete detachment from the patient. Because of this need for detachment, it is very difficult to dowse for someone who is very close, unless we are able to obtain a high degree of objectivity.

DOWSING FOR COLOUR THERAPY

When one thinks about dowsing, the picture that comes to mind is of a person holding a rod or forked stick (as in Figure 5.4). This rod or forked stick is held loosely in both hands. The person then walks over the field or area where he or she has been asked to

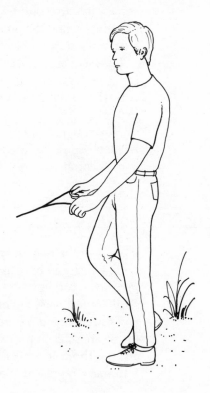

Figure 5.4 Dowsing

locate water, minerals, oil or metals. When the source of whatever is being looked for is located, the rod will move in an upward or downward direction. Having located the source, he or she can then determine, by asking, the quality and amount that is present. If it is water they can ask how pure it is. A good dowser can find out, down to the minutest detail, everything that he or she needs to know.

To dowse is an art which uses the sensitivity of people's awareness and clear thinking. A clear question will always respond to yes or no; when the formulation of a question is not clear, bewilderment – 'I don't know' – follows, so you have to formulate a clear question such as: 'Is there a spring in this field?' As the dowser enters there is either yes or no. If no, he will have to go to the next field. When yes the next question is: 'Is it straight ahead towards the opposite gate.' If yes, he will go and at one point the rod will react. The next question becomes: 'How deep is the spring? 'Is it 10ft?' No reaction again. 'Is it 17ft?' Yes, the reaction is telling that at 17ft there is a spring. Next question: 'How much water per hour? 60 gall? 40 gall? Is it pure; is it lasting?' etc. This becomes so exact that a very clear, detailed and precise knowledge comes up. In colour therapy we can now, by many years of experience, find the precise colours which are needed to harmonize a person's state of health.

Dowsers are used more widely than is generally known. They can save farmers and industry, to name but a few, a lot of money with their skill. It is even possible to locate lost property by this method.

Dowsing can also be used to locate problems in a human being. Human beings are themselves a field of energy in which the spine is the central source.

THE HYGEIA SPINE CHART

If we take the human spine and include the eight flat bones of the skull, which can be looked upon as metamorphosed vertebrae, this gives us a total of 40 vertebrae. But, these eight flat bones of the skull are not used in colour therapy.

The remaining 32 are used and these are divided equally into 4 major areas, each area represented by 8 vertebrae. The 7 cervical and 1st thoracic represent the mental aspect of a person. The next 8 thoracic represent the emotional area. The remaining 3 thoracic

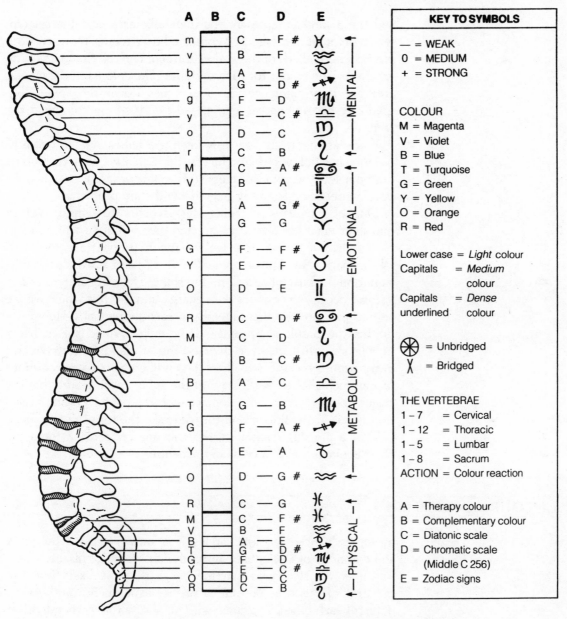

	A	**B**	**C**		**D**		**E**	
	m		C	—	F	#		MENTAL
	v		B	—	F			
	b		A	—	E			
	t		G	—	D	#		
	g		F	—	D			
	y		E	—	C	#		
	o		D	—	C			
	r		C	—	B			
	M		C	—	A	#		
	V		B	—	A			
	B		A	—	G	#		EMOTIONAL
	T		G	—	G			
	G		F	—	F	#		
	Y		E	—	F			
	O		D	—	E			
	R		C	—	D	#		
	M		C	—	D			
	V		B	—	C	#		
	B		A	—	C			METABOLIC
	T		G	—	B			
	G		F	—	A	#		
	Y		E	—	A			
	O		D	—	G	#		
	R		C	—	G			
	M		C	—	F	#		PHYSICAL
	V		B	—	F			
	B		A	—	E			
	T		G	—	D	D	#	
	G		F	—	D	C		
	Y		E	—	D	C	#	
	O		D	—	C	B		
	R		C	—	B			

KEY TO SYMBOLS

— = WEAK
0 = MEDIUM
+ = STRONG

COLOUR
M = Magenta
V = Violet
B = Blue
T = Turquoise
G = Green
Y = Yellow
O = Orange
R = Red

Lower case = *Light* colour
Capitals = *Medium* colour
Capitals underlined = *Dense* colour

⊕ = Unbridged
✕ = Bridged

THE VERTEBRAE
1 – 7 = Cervical
1 – 12 = Thoracic
1 – 5 = Lumbar
1 – 8 = Sacrum
ACTION = Colour reaction

A = Therapy colour
B = Complementary colour
C = Diatonic scale
D = Chromatic scale
     (Middle C 256)
E = Zodiac signs

Responses which have been made

M									
E									
ME									
PH									

M – mental; ME – metabolic; E – emotional; PH – physical

Name of Client ——————————

Date of Chart —————— Made by —————— (Signed)

Treatment Colour ——————

Figure 5.5 The Medical Colour Diagnosis Chart

and the 5 lumbar represent the metabolic area, and the sacrum, which before it became fused contained 8 vertebrae, represents the physical body. Each of these 4 sections contain the 8 colours of the spectrum, one colour for each vertebra. The colours in the mental area are very light, but as one comes down the spine they gradually become darker, ending with very strong colours in the sacrum.

If we, as therapists, are dowsing for a fellow human being in order to try and help them, the first thing that we have to do is to raise our level of consciousness to the state where we are able to become detached from our personal and daily problems.

One of the ways of doing this is firstly to confirm within ourselves what our intentions are and then to light a white candle on behalf of the work that we are about to undertake. We then take a chart of the human spine (Figure 5.5) and ask the patient to sign it on the back of and along the spine. Their signature acts as a witness because it contains their energy and it is this which we are able to pick up. We then dowse out each individual vertebra. To do this, the middle finger of the non-dominant hand is used. Most people are right-handed so they use the left hand. Raising the arm away from the chest, we allow the middle finger to hover about half an inch above the diagram of the spine, making sure that the finger does not come into contact with the paper. Where a reaction is felt in the finger, and this can take the form of pain, heat, cold or a prickling sensation, the relevant vertebra on the spine chart is marked with a cross in the centre.

COLOUR COUNSELLING

In very advanced scientific circles, it is known that the thoughts and emotions of a scientist control the end result of his/her work. The finer the structures that they use, the more likely that the outcome of the same absolutely precise experiment, can be very different each time it is conducted. This shows that each individual person has exact, individual harmony patterns which are not acceptable to anyone else.

Colour therapy is based on many of these ideas and can often be proved. When we learn to visualize, to sense the effects of colour, learn to think colour, then we can create certain experiences. When there is conflict between people and one of them visualizes a deep strong blue into this conflict, it is quite often

*Figure 5.6 Projecting
Colour in the Pattern of a
Figure of Eight*

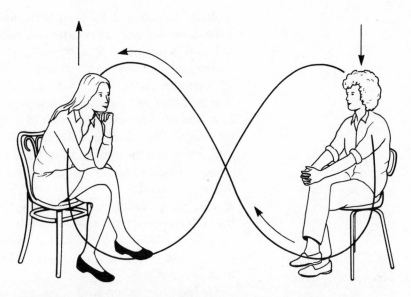

The person who transmits the healing is first drawing in from the higher self
the energies which are then offered to the person who needs this help.
Through this action the 'patient' is related back to his/her own higher self
and finds a refreshing healing occurs.

surprising how quickly the conflict dissolves. Conflict comes out of
misunderstanding. When we are challenged on this we become
insecure and try to defend ourselves. This causes tension which in
turn causes contraction within the body. The colour associated
with contraction is red. Blue is the colour of expansion and
relaxation and this is the reason why this colour causes the conflict
to dissolve.

If a person is aware of tension in a fellow human being, they can
restore peace and calm in this being by visualizing the colour of
blue and projecting it out in the pattern of a figure of eight to the
person in need of help (see Figure 5.6).

As A sends the energy of blue through B, all of B's negative
energy is anchored and the uplifting effect which the blue energy
contains brings calm and ease to B. This can only be done successfully if A exercises detachment and is working purely for the good
of B and not for his/her own self-esteem. What is projected from B
is acknowledged and anchored on the low point of the figure of
eight. This ensures that no negativity is returned to A. This is a
technique of silent communication and, according to the energies

wished for, can also be used with other colours. All those who have done this will know how successful it is.

I was a member of a training group run by a leader who challenged each one of us to express the way in which we work with people. A chaplain, who was part of this group, complained that he never got very much response from the people whom he interviewed. The leader asked him to explain how he started his interviews. The chaplain described very clearly his procedure. He said that when the person sat in front of him, into his mind would come thoughts such as: this is 'Aunty', 'Charlie', 'The Joker', 'Misery Guts' etc.

The group leader then challenged the chaplain to give each of the sixteen people in the group a title. The chaplain was delighted by this and successfully went half way round the circle when he came to me. He looked at me and said: 'Oh, this is Alladin and I trust him not.'

He then moved on to the young woman who was next to me and said: 'She is "benevolent" mum.'

At this point the chaplain broke down in tears and could not continue. The leader allowed a little time for him to regain his composure. During this time, from where I was sitting, I made a figure of eight, sending calm and relaxation to him. Obviously, no one knew what I was doing. The leader then asked the chaplain to choose from the group two people whom he would like to counsel him and help him to find a new technique for his interviews. The chaplain chose 'benevolent mum' and myself whom he had previously said he did not trust.

Many more such cases could be quoted. But, what one has to remember is that this technique must never be used for self-advantage.

It cannot be said often enough that the moment you use any therapy, you become the channel for the energy of that therapy to flow from your higher self through you. When you apply this to a fellow human being, you are under a very strict obligation to observe all your own thoughts, feelings and actions (again a threefold principle). All the training and all the learning, together with the practical work which was done during your study, have become your expertise. Like a good pianist, you no longer have to think how to apply, on the practical side, your method of healing. Your fingers, arms and the use of the instruments, lamps or coloured sheets are in your cell memory. This means that this part of your work has become automatic, leaving space in your thoughts to interpret what is happening between you and your patient.

I use the word 'interpret' because you are no longer using your intellect, you are using your intuition to sense the interplay between you and your patient. The colours which you apply are active energies. They are working to bring a harmonious balance to the patient. However, each single application, each hour, day, time and meeting is a new experience and the events which they bring are unique. You may repeat what you have done so many times before. But each treatment can, and indeed does, unlock new doors for both the patient and therapist. The therapist is the specialist who has to interpret what is now happening.

Observe, listen, sense, perceive, as if you were watching a play in the theatre. Make notes of what you feel is happening and at the appropriate moment, express to the patient what you have perceived. During a treatment a patient can enter into a new stage of his/her being. All good therapists are conscious of what they can use to bring about a good treatment.

At the correct time, a point will be reached when all circumstances meet together.

The time is right.
The patient is ready to open up to the treatment.
The therapist becomes in this moment a perfect channel and suddenly something happens which the patient and the therapist have 'waited for'.

Such moments are very special and the patient has received and accepted aspects of healing that before this moment were not possible. Yes, miracles can happen when, as described above, the time is right. At such a moment, the following dedication, which the therapist can use, has been fully realized.

'I am in the right place
At the right time
For the right purpose.'

Chapter 6

THE HEALING LIGHT

*. . . and the light shone into darkness and the darkness comprehended it
not . . .*

John 1 v: 1)

PIGMENT AND ILLUMINATION: ADDITIVE AND SUBTRACTIVE COLOURS

We have in the preceding chapters explored light, colours and
talked about darkness. And there has been an underlying assump-
tion that light and colour are all registered through the eyes. But
to see with the sense of sight is only one part of our seeing
capacity: our eyes are only part of this sense. We have referred to
the fact that all our cells are light-sensitive and that the human
body is transparent; that the pigments of our skin, our organs
and even our bones are not insensitive to the changes of
day and night, although we have to measure this using degrees
of opaqueness.

If you can, go into a small room where there is only one small
window. Close the door and put a black piece of paper over
the window so that it is absolutely dark. Cut a hole in the
paper no bigger than the palm of your hand. On a bright
sunny day, cover this hole with your hand and very soon
you will find that a very small orange light is created as you
look at this patch which you have covered. This is actually
the complementary colour to the daylight blue of early
afternoon.

The most healing light is the daylight because it contains the full spectrum. 'Full spectrum' means that all the visible range of light is part of the illumination. It holds all the colours in it, but because it is so bright, it is often said to be white light.

Shine a red light on to a white screen or wall. Add to this a blue light partly overlapping the red light. Now add a green light which partly overlaps the first two. At the point where all three overlap, you will not get a mixture of the three colours but a white light (see Figure 6.1).

Each coloured light which is added to the existing lights will make the area lighter and in the end create white light, although only red, blue and green filters are used. For this you will need the following: three torches, one of each of the following colour filters (which Hygeia can supply; these are of high quality and are not cheap): blue, red, green; you may also add orange, yellow, violet, etc.; a white screen some 24in × 20in and washing pegs. Black out your room and see how your colours are mixing.

If you repeat this using paint or crayons, the place where all three colours overlap will now become a very dark area and not white as experienced with light (see Figure 6.2).

Each pigment adds further darkness to the existing pigments of the other. This only becomes clear when you work with water colours which are transparent.

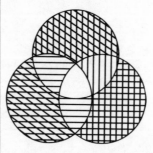

Figure 6.1 The Subtractive Colours

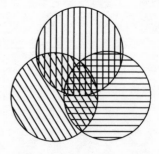

Figure 6.2 The Additive Colours

ARTIFICIAL LIGHT

The quality of light is a very important issue and we owe a great deal of gratitude to Dr John Ott for this awareness.

Over many years, we researched into the reactions of all living things to fluorescent light. I knew the scientist, Dr Hans Heitler who developed fluorescent light in the early 1930s. When he developed it he pronounced that it was not a healthy light, labelling it as emergency illumination only. In all cases of artificial light we must ask ourselves the question: is it healthy? If the answer is no, then a better quality light, which will be more expensive, will in the long run turn out to be cheaper in terms of health preservation.

Dr John Ott took Heitler's work and found that an improvement is possible when the hue and the very basic production method are carefully considered. From this, John Ott developed a full spectrum tube which has no colour distortions. Artificial light which has been developed for economical reasons does not take into consideration its effect upon the mental, emotional and even physical well-being of people who are subjected to it.

We know that light and behaviour patterns are very closely linked. The colour of light has a very special effect when we take into consideration its complementary colour which always appears in its own shadow. For example, if a yellow light is shone on to a tree, the shadow produced by that tree would appear as violet. The purity of the light shone on the tree ascertains the purity of its shadow colour. Coloured shadows can be very deceptive, but also very beautiful.

Absolute light and absolute shadow do not exist since these concepts are always relative. However, where light and shadow, day and night meet – in morning and evening – we can experience colours. The blue end of the spectrum appears in the morning and the red end during sunset. Man can extract from nature that which he deems useful to his ends. Whether this is beneficial or detrimental depends very much on the motives and purpose behind any development.

Our society needs artificial light. One or two hours of power cuts soon teach us that we may not have a meal, hear music (or background noise), see our way around the space we occupy, that we must do without heating and often lose track of time. We suddenly sink to a standard of living even lower than that of our great-grandparents since we mostly live in homes where there is no hearth, no fireplace and, in buildings with air conditioning, no natural air. Thus we become slaves to our modern civilization. However, we may now appreciate what electricity can do for us.

Edison, the inventor of our household tungsten lamp, left us for many decades with a standard colour of illumination which contains a high red content. Much changed with the advent of fluorescent light. This gave us a very bright light at a much reduced energy cost since the greater part of the electric current is converted into light and not heat. Society has a great need for economy and fluorescent light sources provide this admirably. Hans Heitler (whom I knew very well) said: 'This is economy light and must not be used in peacetime.' This warning has not been adhered to and we have subjected a whole generation to a light source which basically can cause stress, whether it be in the office, or in public places such as shops and stores, or from street lighting.

The reason why this causes stress is because fluorescent light is based on a gas filament and not on an alloy glowing one. The AC (alternating current) has a cycle of 50 to 50 on/off vibration. The human eye cannot see this fast flicker. However, the nerve ends of the skin pick it up subconsciously, which causes the brain and nervous system to vibrate in a mechanical rhythm. It causes headaches, deterioration of eyesight and general stress.

During the 1970s and early 1980s we developed, with the help of a very good international firm, a component which is now known as the Electronic Ballast, and which has removed the unhealthy 'flicker' from the fluorescent tube. In this way, we are no longer subjected to the detrimental 50hz flicker of ordinary fluorescent lights. The cheaper, poor illumination which we generally install may well have to be paid for later in repairing the damage to health.

It is thanks to Dr John Ott that we have the full spectrum fluorescent tubes available today. All of these, with the exception of eight-foot tubes, can be operated by electronic ballast. Daylight is endowed with full spectrum frequency and electronically ballasted full spectrum tubes produce near-perfect light for all biochemical structures, plants, animals and humans.

My company has been concerned with colour and its effect on living structure since 1956, when, as its founder, I first investigated colours and their use for human health in a small cellar near Bristol. Since different colours vibrate at different frequencies, the effect of colours on people also varies and can be positive or negative in character. The red end of the spectrum has a frequency of about

4.6 x 10^{14} and causes contraction in all biochemical structures. The blue end, with a frequency of about 7.5 x 10^{14}, causes expansion. Red, in other words, causes excitement, stress, high blood pressure and tension. All green objects become black under red illumination, and all red objects become white.

PUBLIC LIGHTING

Low-pressure sodium light turns most colours into dirty greys and khaki. Thus the night scene in a city street with this monochromatic sodium light creates a very negative environment for the inhabitants. The shadows of this light are a dirty maroon-grey. Violet, its beautiful clear neighbour in the spectrum, is the colour of dignity and respect and when this is distorted into the unclean colour of a muddy maroon-grey, it evokes psychological responses that cause people without positive motivations or plans to adopt an attitude of violent destructive craving. While sexuality can be the highest form of human dignified expression, it can in such an environment, become the lowest and most desecrated activity. Records show that in areas where education has failed to create a worthwhile mode of daily life, such 'floundering' people are easily provoked to destroy positive activities and objects which are, to them, a challenge they cannot live up to. Sex crimes of the most unpleasant kind can be the result of this.

Street lighting is monochromatic and causes depression and disoriented humans without positivity who quite frequently are under the influence of drink, smoking and often drugs. For all those who can no longer live a worthwhile existence, this kind of lighting creates in their emotions and subconscious a tendency to 'drag down' all that is still positive in them. They are often not alone in their suffering, having others whom they have forced into this negative state. Gang leaders need weak followers whom they can bully.

There is no justification in describing the above phenomenon unless we can come up with a helping hand to improve matters. Improvements looked upon with a long-term view may require some investments which do not immediately pay off. They should not, therefore, be considered as an emergency measure. Invest now and it will grow into a better future where fewer offences are committed and the police, guardians of order, are better supported. A street light in which the spectrum of light is more towards the blue end would be ideal, but any increase towards better colour rendition and full spectrum illumination can be seen as helpful, as we have discussed before.

Blue is the colour of relaxation and peace; with blue, blood pressure is lowered and slow movement is induced, stress is taken out and violence greatly reduced. In 1974 I made two suggestions to the police: that they should create blue-lit exit tunnels from football grounds through which all spectators would have to pass on leaving, or that arenas should have a secondary illumination circuit which would flood the arena with blue light towards the end of the match. As far as I know, neither suggestion has been taken up and the violence and hysteria at some matches have led to the loss of human lives.

COLOUR AND EFFECT

Basically, light creates new ambiences and is able to change an environment just as theatrical lighting changes the mood on stage. Artificial illumination creates vast pockets of shadow; shadow areas cause challenges to the human mind and emotions. The colour of such shadows invites certain activities which one could say are lured out of emotions and become urges. Undirected people are finally provoked into turning these urges into actions.

Very fine degrees of a mixture of shades can change the meanings of colour to the individual person. These meanings cannot be put into concepts, and far less into words.

Psychological reactions to colour stem mainly from the psyche of the individual person. The complexity of each mind ensures a very personal appraisal of colour and therefore it is not easy to make generalizations beyond what has been outlined above. However, through the thirty years of my research, I can say that on the whole the following effects can be experienced. Colours impress children very strongly as they are, both boys and girls, very pliable. A colour seen and experienced together with a very happy moment can remain for decades a favourite colour. Equally, a bad moment associated with another colour in early years can remain negative for an equally long time.

The conscious acceptance of a bad experience can solve negative attitudes and a 'bad' colour can become agreeable. Any experience, whether mental or emotional, can introduce itself into our health pattern and thus become a physical change, thereby altering our well-being. This can lead to disease as well as to health.

It would be quite a study to examine all night crimes in terms of the light and shadow present at the scene of each crime. It has become fashionable to experiment with different colours in both the decoration and illumination of rooms. The prison cell painted pink, which is said to calm down violent behaviour, has a very extreme backlash. The biochemical structure is forced into an extreme order to which it is not normally subjected. Pink is nearest to magenta, the first colour that emerges out of ultra-violet. It promotes change, letting go, dissolving, giving up. Out of these qualities comes the relaxation out of violent behaviour. Afterwards, however, there is a backlash of intense rebellion and violence. So what have we achieved? The colour manipulation has been applied through our intellect without the philosophy of the principles to back it up. The pink cell is, therefore, not actually a treatment in terms of an improvement in the person who is subjected to the pink. It is an emergency action and, like a bad chess player, we have not taken into account the ensuing moves of our opponent.

Man has a double nature: one which is rational, logical, orderly and creates reason; the other intuitive, artisitic, playful and which cannot be contained in strictly reasonable terms. We also have to take into account our nervous system; the brain has two halves, one mathematical (left side) and the other intuitive and artistic (right side). In our present educational system, far too much emphasis is still placed on the mathematical and logical side. We neglect the intuitive which contains all the arts, music, painting, drama, etc. Many young people miss out at school as they are not mentally suited to academic work. They become failures and end up with no place in society. As they become vulnerable to all the influences of the environment, they become increasingly at odds with a society they have failed to please, and often turn to crime, especially in the deprived city areas. But ultimately they are saying through this behaviour to society, 'I am also here. Acknowledge me.'

Any light, including street lighting, always manipulates a response. If it is well designed and based on deeper understanding, it will influence people towards better behaviour. The colour of light plays a vital part in this. The perfect colour would be daylight equivalent, full-spectrum. In other words, blue light such as in daylight tubes. The incandescent lamp has one great advantage:

Figure 6.3 Incandescent,
Fluorescent and 'Perfect'
Light Patterns

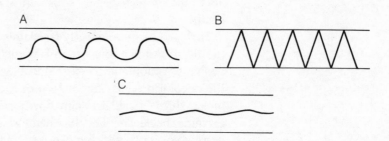

'A' is the incandescent lamp, 'B' is the unprotected, not electronically ballasted, fluorescent lamp or tube. 'C' is the 'perfect' light which we can now have.

it never goes fully out nor fully on. The effect is a cycle between on and off which does not touch the extreme on either side (see Figure 6.3).

Reams have been written, proved and contradicted, arguments have been staged over methods and the use of light in industry, commerce and entertainment. Yet there is a deep-down feeling of what is right and wrong. This has been built into and passed on to our cell structure for millennia. This deep-down cell memory tells us that light is vibrating at a constant frequency. In other words, at such a high frequency of the electro-magnetic spectrum that it goes into quintillions of vibrations per second. Perhaps one should say that the finest of all human sensitivity can only recognize it as a calming, steady light which burns without interruption.

Any rhythm we put into this has an effect upon us. Therefore, we must find out what should be the correct rhythm. And there is always the promise of constant, life-enhancing energy which does not let us down by a sudden on/off action. Nothing can be perfect, that we must accept. The point is that we do now have at our disposal means to ensure much better lighting conditions. We could ensure that stress through lighting is at a minimum and that work and leisure can be experienced by way of colour at a calm and peaceful level. This will, in turn, improve work output, quality of work, and the elimination of errors which occur within seconds and can take hours to correct.

The colour of light slips very quickly into the subconscious cell memory, whereas the colour in decoration stays with us mentally. These two can, and must, be used in conjunction with each other when interior design is to be successful. Since we have within us the complementary reactions of our brain functions, and since we are on this planet as men and women (i.e. two complementary energies), this principle of duality must be adopted so as to harmonize the environment and through it improve human communications. So we use light in a very subtle way, with a very carefully chosen colour and the well-considered decoration of living and working space. Very high illumination levels cause non-communication among groups of people.

Much research still has to be done before we can come up with a constructive design. The balance has always to be redressed, for in it lies the emergence of harmonious intercommunication for the purpose of increasing life's benefits and for the sake of real lighting development which will benefit all concerned.

Those professionals who may be in charge of illumination should increase their understanding of what good colour lighting can achieve.

THE WATER SOLARISER

When we become sufficiently aware that colour and light together can help us to be more harmonious and support our health, then we can ask how these can be employed to help us. An old and very well-known way to bring colour into the body was, and still is, practised in ayurvedic medicine.

Very simply, cover a glass of spring water all round with quality colour glass and expose this to daylight for an hour when the sun is shining or two to three hours on a cloudy day (see Figure 6.4). By doing this you will change the chemical make-up of the water. Red glass will cause the water to taste slightly sour, and blue glass makes the same quality of water taste sweetish. The red-treated water has an energizing effect if taken regularly; say a few sips every ten minutes. It will make you feel more active. The blue water will relax you, and thus you can begin to help yourself. Realize, however, that these methods are gentle and therefore cause a gradual alteration and not an abrupt one.

Figure 6.4 The Water Solariser

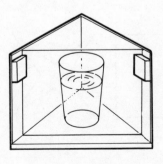

You can use any of the colours of the rainbow to solarize your spring water. To help with arthritic conditions, use yellow glass, green for cleansing, turquoise to strengthen your immune system etc. Refer to the chart in Chapter 3 to find the colour needed for a specific complaint. Do not lose patience when working with this method. Your 'problem' has come gradually and gradually it will go away.

The colours cause responses within us and the eye-strengthening chart shown in Chapter 3 can be extended to include all the rainbow colours. This is done with the aid of the 'Colour Consciousness' set (see Figure 6.5). This set contains 24 plates which, when worked with, help your memory. It contains very special geometric shapes, linking it to mathematics and thereby appealing to the brain functions. Our Western education is left-brain orientated and this causes people to learn to judge, to calculate often to their own advantage, regardless of their environment as a whole, but more seriously affecting society when used against your fellow human person. Beauty and art, colours and their energies appeal to the right side of the brain, the intuitive, imaginative energies within us. By putting together colour and form (shapes) in a meaningful sequence we can again create harmony by using regularly such a sequence as a tool to enliven our own being.

Colours as you now know are linked to their complementary colours. This phenomena is not only restricted to colour but

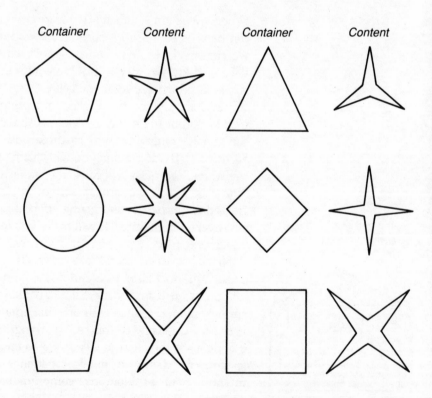

Figure 6.5 The Colour Consciousness Set

Figure 6.6 (From left to right) The Colour Space Illuminator, The Pure Light Lamp, and The Artists' and Designers' Lamp

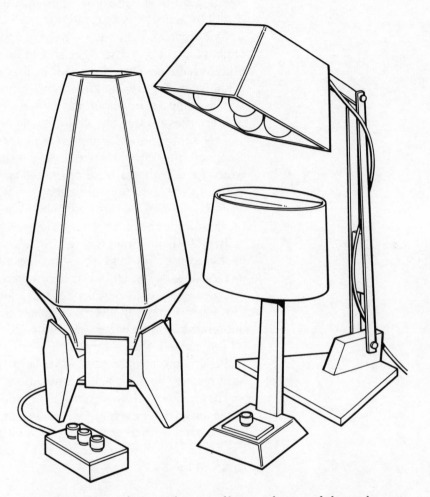

reappears also in form. When working with any of the eight sets, you are continuously activating both the left and right side of the brain.

The complementary colour range should by now be well known to you. The same principle is, however, experienced when we examine forms. Forms have complementary forms by way of their tension energy. Each edge of a form has a given tension but the more powerful tension is the diagonal, to start with, not seen, but experienced.

Your brain is not a heap of cells of which you use only one-tenth, as it is said, but a very fine organ which responds to your consciousness level and you can be in charge of the activities of these cells. The crossing from one side of the brain to the other is bringing more life into your thought capacity, enabling you gradually to improve your creativity.

Our sense of sight has in this day and age to cope with many negative aspects and so light should be of good quality. Hygeia Studios have developed a good reading and working lamp which is known as the Hygeia Pure Light Lamp (see Figure 6.6).

This lamp is an important source of illumination for artists, printers, dressmakers and all those who are concerned with colour.

This light is far less tiring on the eyes than the usual light; eye strain often occurs when one is constantly under illumination which has a high incidence of the red spectrum in it. The muscles in the iris are, with normal lighting, in slight tension all the time.

Strip lighting or fluorescent tube lighting is in varying degrees more or less harmful to the eyes. A full spectrum 'tube' has gone halfway to help. However, the AC electricity current still leaves us, because of the highly responsive vapour, with the hitherto unavoidable flicker. Until this is completely corrected, one should not be subjected to this light for any length of time. To correct this, we now have an electronic ballast which causes full spectrum fluorescent light to become a very high quality illumination.

The Hygeia Pure Light Lamp offers a relaxing illumination while also producing a clear, true light. The actual colour of the light relaxes the eyes, while conventional light creates tension.

Those who read, write, sew, embroider or do any colour work in the long winter evenings will soon learn to appreciate this lamp.

The lamp is fitted with a dimmer switch which not only allows the light to be gently controlled, but saves the bulbs and causes no shock to the user.

THE COLOUR SPACE ILLUMINATOR

Do we always need to be in a given illumination which we cannot alter or can we think of another colour to be surrounded by? This question was raised in the early years of our research and through it the Colour Space Illuminator was born. This is a lamp whose colours can be changed and mixed according to the wish of the user (see Figure 6.6).

The Colour Space Illuminator is not only a beautiful object with infinite colour and brightness changes, but it is also the means by which the owner can benefit in health.

Blue is used for calming and lowering blood pressure, relief of asthma and general relaxation; violet to feel uplifted; orange when depressed; red for energy and for raising blood pressure.

The lamp creates an atmosphere for massage, conversation, or listening to music; a happy light as a general background, or soothing for children who have difficulties in sleeping.

Green light is the only light which is excluded because we feel that it is not a safe colour in the hands of the untrained person.

It is recommended that the actual use for this instrument for therapy is about 3 × 15–20 minutes per week, and that during this time no other activity should be undertaken. One should be either dressed completely in white or undressed.

Most people take light and illumination for granted and do not realize the major contribution it makes to people's physical and emotional well-being or disorders. Within human beings are natural rhythms aligned to their natural environment. Basically we require daylight to stimulate our senses (activity), and a natural darkness to give relaxation (sleep). People who work in a highly lit environment should also spend a lot of time in darkness.

In the technological world of today, we are being forcibly divorced from our natural rhythms. Broadly speaking, the agricultural workers are the only people whose work allows them to remain aligned to their environment. Millions of people working in offices and factories can only feel the influences of natural light at short, odd intervals during the day. A considerable number of

---

The Colour-Silk Treatment

How about treating yourself to a wonderful experience?

Undress and lie down in a light, warm bedroom with music of your choice playing quietly in the background. Select one of the colours of the rainbow in the form of a beautiful full-length silk and cover your whole body with it. It is important that you use pure natural fibre such as cotton, wool or silk. The very best material is silk. Stay for at least twenty minutes in this position, allowing yourself to listen to the music and to daydream. You might also like to use one of the meditations from Chapter I. (These are available on tape from Hygeia Studios).

people on night work, or working underground, are not afforded even the odd interval. Such a divorce considerably undermines our chance of well-being. It is further undermined through our being subjected to artificial lighting which, almost invariably, has been installed by people who do not know about its adverse effects physically or emotionally.

THE STAGE REPORT

A fully trained colour practitioner is able to broadcast a treatment to a patient. This has proven to be successful because the spine chart which has been made for a person acts as a communication of very special energy transmission.

When the wireless (radio) was discovered, it became possible to send sound waves over a radius of ever greater distances to any receiver from a transmitter. We now take this fact for granted and use it everywhere in the world; for peaceful, military and medical purposes.

In that band of frequencies, at a higher rate, we break into the colour spectrum which belongs to the electro-magnetic spectrum. Within it are contained X-rays and, much higher up still, radium waves.

We can transmit colour not only through the TV network but also from a human transmitter to a human receiver. All these technical feats have come out of the human mind. The human, however, contains far greater capacities.

Colour therapy acts in this way. The human instrument learns how to transmit and receive accurate information between the therapist and the patient. Colour is then transmitted by way of light through high-quality filters after a diagnostic spine chart has been made. Through the making of this chart, some colours are transmitted to the patient. Treatment with the patient present and absent treatment literally work hand in hand.

Some of the conditions that we can treat in the above way are migraine, asthma, stress, AIDS, cancer, inflammatory conditions, autism, mental, emotional and metabolic problems. It must be remembered that colour therapy, like all medical treatment, can only be successful if the patient (a) comes to us in good time, and (b) wants to co-operate and is willing to change his/her general lifestyle. This may include thought (mental activity), feelings (emotions), diet and the physical daily rhythms of the day.

We are all apt to neglect part of our person and sometimes for such long periods that disease can enter into our system. If we do not communicate with ourselves, we find that some of the functions go into recession and through this stop functioning. Many diseases can be caused these days by interference with human functions. Epilepsy can be caused through strobe lights and autism through a malfunction in the administration of a general anaesthetic.

This does not mean that the medical side of it is wrong but only that the individual person reacts very specially according to his/her own life patterns. Whereas in almost all cases these patterns conform, occasionally they do not and no one can be blamed.

In the past, electro-convulsive therapy tried to repair mental conditions. It has now gone out of fashion because it has been unable to reach the spiritual part of man, which makes a cure very doubtful. We as colour therapists claim no cures but are thankful when we find improvements have occurred through our treatment.

SCANNING

Scanning as a healing art is one of the most powerful types of healing which we can use. This was known and used in ancient temple rituals, but with the advent of the mechanical and machine age much of this knowledge has been lost.

In brief, whoever comes for this art of healing is asked to wear natural fibres such as cotton, silk or wool and to be dressed in white. If they are not dressed in white then a gown is provided for them.

To be able to develop the sensitivity of our own instruments, our bodies, we must be aware that we are composed of the spiritual, the soul and the physical bodies; all of these are incorporated into us as human beings. This acknowledgement is really important as we develop our being more and more and it must be from this viewpoint that one welcomes a patient.

Furthermore, we are also an aura being, an etheric being and a sensual being. The aura field, the most sensitive field, not yet visible to many, carries for us the energies which cause our body to be well or not so well. The etheric body (much smaller than the aura) is close to the physical body of flesh and blood. This etheric body carries the response mechanism from our physical body into

Another method of working with colour is with stained glass and quartz crystals. Place the stained-glass filter over a small lamp. This needs to be designed so that a good air flow is incorporated into it for cooling. Good quality stained glass is very expensive and very easily broken by heat. Place on to the lamp the coloured filter of your choice and then place on top of the filter the quartz crystal. The crystal will now be saturated with your chosen colour. The crystal needs to remain on the filter for at least 20 minutes. After this interval of time, you can place the solarised crystal on to any part of your body where you feel the colour that you have chosen is needed. This part of your body will gently absorb the crystal-colour energy.

the life body which is highly spiritually, magnetically and electrically charged.

The therapist can usually tell from this method where there are any deficiencies in the organism of a person and colour, heat and magnetism are sensed. The healing that follows can be very powerful.

As we grow more and more aware, so we will become conscious of new uses in colour and find ever finer experiences for the use of colour. We must remember that all outer work, both in science and in art, must eventually be brought into the inner mind and become not only a factual memory but also a part of our own being.

In all the efforts which you make to maintain your health, you must remember that here, on this planet, we are subject to the five original elements. These are: earth (green), the matter on which we base and indeed hold together our liquid state. This state is the second element, water (blue). The third element is the warmth body which is related to fire (red); the fourth, our gaseous body which is air (yellow). The given colours for these elements go back to the original teachings of Hippocrates 475bc. There is, however, a fifth element which is essential to life and is called ether (violet). It is contained in all the above four (by which these are alive, containing life force or ether), but ether is also an element in its own right. When we work on health, it is very helpful to see these elements as actual beings. In the next chapter, therefore, we shall examine how to work with these beings, ourselves, and the vast cosmic beings known as angels.

Chapter 7

ELEMENTS, HUMANS AND ANGELS

Each soul is potentially divine.
The goal is to manifest this divinity within by
controlling nature, external and internal:
Do this either by work, or worship or psychic
control, or philosophy. By one, or more, or all
of these and be free.
This is the whole of religion, doctrines or dogmas,
or rituals, or books, or temples, or forms, are but
of secondary details

Swami Vivekananda, *Raja Yoga*
(Advaita Ashrama S Dehli, Calcutta 14)

THE PLAN FOR THE PLANET

The human race has gone to sleep and has lost the consciousness about the real worlds which should make a complete unit. Children, who are born knowing of this wholeness, are not given confirmation of what they bring down with them from the invisible worlds.

In the teaching of this present age, parents and teachers are only concerned with technology and what children need to know in order to build better and bigger calculators and computers. This leads in the end to a race who can no longer think in a holistic way and all memories of the vast coherence of all wisdom and knowledge becomes blurred.

Behind the whole of the visible world are invisible energies which allow the visible world to appear. Out of these cosmic-galactic fields are poured into this earth the spiritual intentions, the plan for which this planet has been chosen and its people selected. The most outstanding task humanity has been given has sadly been forgotten and such activities completely neglected. What was given to mankind was the dominion over the elements and the kingdoms of nature. This sevenfold realm over which mankind is to preside is earth, water, fire, air; and mineral, plant and animal. There is a further way that these can be seen, in terms of the elements and the kingdoms. The denser minerals (crystals) stand outside the other elements in the same way as humans stand outside the other kingdoms.

The mineral world	earth	green
The liquid world	water	blue
The warmth world	fire	red
The gaseous world	air	yellow
The kingdom of the mineral world	crystals	white/magenta

When we relax our mind and slow down the levels of consciousness, we 'plunge' into states of awareness where the inner-vision colours change from the normal awareness into certain biorhythms (see Maxwell Cade, *The Awakened Mind*). By controlling brain pulse speed, an inner experience of colours, in a very well-known pattern, occurs: the norm, about 30–12, pulses is simply multicolour, and therefore not experienced as 'colour'. Slow down, by becoming very still and relaxed: a kind of blue appears which spreads down to about 7 brain pulses. After this it is advisable to have guidance and not experiment without instruction; but between 7–4 pulses gold is experienced. After 4–1 pulse per second an almost white occurs. But do be warned: do not experiment without professional training. It can unbalance the mind.

When we look at the above colours and see that the kingdoms are composed of the elements, there is an added order and the colours come to be experienced.

The kingdom of the plants	gold
The kingdom of the animals	indigo
The kingdom of humans	multicolour (Beta rhythms)
The kingdom of etheric energy	violet

Yes, the etheric kingdom deserves the same care which was meant to be given to the preceding realms. The intention is to offer to all that exists, *thanks, blessings and love*. Not at the command of only one, not because we are made to do it, not under any pressure from anywhere. For this purpose the fruit of the Tree of Knowledge was taken so that we might become grown ups. We were children, but we should now grow to become sons and daughters of God.

We have made many mistakes, but we are learning. We are finding the way to know that deep in our hearts we choose to thank, to bless and to give undemanded and unlimited love. In other words, we do this out of absolute freedom, out of our own free choice, knowing that this is the only creative way. In doing this we will learn to love every thing, regardless of to which of the seven kingdoms it belongs. Deep inside the visible kingdoms there are very powerful beings just as behind the invisible, spiritual worlds there are very mighty angels and eternal masters.

The whole of the mineral world is subdivided into crystals, metals and sedimentary rock. In days gone by, the wise women and men would talk about the beings who are locked in these molecules and called them the Gnomes. They give the solidity on which we depend in order to stand on a firm earth. Next we will have to see the rivers, the lakes and oceans and recognize within this water element the Undines. Then we become aware of the warmth of earth, the glow which is inside the mountains, the fire and the light. Responsible for this are the Salamanders. Finally the element of air, the breath of life and all the gaseous energy. Inside each of these molecules are the Sylphs. There is, however, a fifth element which stands in its own right and it penetrates the other four, giving to them life.

We can take all things apart and reduce them to their clinical and material components but they no longer have any life. It is almost like taking apart a clock: it will stop ticking. Perhaps ether is the spring wound carefully by the master; it is the force within, but so fine in nature that it can 'move' all things, the growth of crystals, plants, animals and humans.

Only when man misuses the given energies by applying his knowledge in selfish ways does the life force of the ether no longer have space. Ether can heal. Behind it stand the cosmic rays which are invisible. It is the realm of the great masters. These beings have many names, all of which limit their universal power. It is therefore wise that they ultimately have no name. They all now wait for mankind to choose the right way so that a new precedent may be introduced and absolute freedom of the true choices is made by which no power is the sole power.

Progress always depends on a new challenge and this challenge has been built into the destiny of earth. It is the duality which always yearns for fulfilment. It is the age-old longing of the two platonic half-spheres where each one looks for the ideal other half to create a new unity. Man as a masculine being only cannot exist, nor can there be only woman.

In the ultimate effort to be independent, each one comes to the point where there are many unanswered questions and too many unexplained riddles. The twofold nature also leads into the three-fold nature, which in itself goes on and on and on.

Out of this, we should see how this principle also applies to the universe. The cosmic-galactic space on the one hand and on the other hand the material world, where we now should find that concealed inside the elements there are again invisible creatures.

Why do we only in extreme need and desperation resort to either or both of the vast kingdom of the angels and the minute kingdom of the elementals? We need to communicate again with these beings. If we do not we shall perish.

Consider the physics of the very small. We again arrive at the point where we have to leave too much unexplained. If we can at this point call these unexplained riddles the elemental beings, those invisible forces within minerals, water, fire and air, we may be led into areas where new answers can be found. Certainly colour leads us into a part of such explanations. Concentration leads by the same principle of polarity (duality) into relaxation, time off, not thinking, not being filled with a content; just as we need sleep after waking. A short period of concentration during research, (being awake), followed by a period of absolute relaxa-tion, forgetting instead of remembering, is a principle of Rudolf Steiner's teaching. Make your mind free of thoughts, concepts and ideas; listen, otherwise you will not hear; look, otherwise you will not see. We need to apply this idea of opposites to every moment in our daily work. Let the fear to forget dissolve into the trust to remember. When you relax, ask the angels and the elemental beings to give you the information which you require now.

To receive such messages, you have to let go, relax and medi-tate. Relax and then receive healing. Relax and then be aware.

THE ELEMENTS

The Element of Earth

The very, very small creatures which we can behold in the mineral world are the Gnomes. These are concealed in the molecule of each cell. The atom's existence is due to the neutron and proton circling round in space and creating the energy which we call 'atom'. This again demonstrates the same principle. Call the proton orange and the neutron blue and you will be able to experience this in colour.

Visualization of colour is one of the most powerful experiences, and we need to use the energy of the complementary colour.

A very fast 'aura' like energy is around all the living kingdoms, whether these are small or large or the whole. This energy is again perceived by those who can 'see' the energy fields, the aura.

Each element, earth, water, fire and air, but also the mineral plant, animal and human kingdom have a kind of 'breathing' pattern. The denser the substance the faster the inflow energy becomes. When ultimately a human person arrives at the stage where he/she can 'breathe' rhythmically in and out then we have the state of consciousness which creates awareness. The more a manifested energy can breathe out the more can the consciousness develop. The principle is that by way of the outflow an energy field is expanded and a counterflow is the inevitable result. The problem only becomes unbearable to those who cannot manage to handle the information received in this way and many end up in mental hospitals where then drugs and ECT are used to control the person's input. Most are indeed then 'vegetables'. Follow this principle and plants still have a great amount of inflow but some outflow measured against the mineral world. See also José, Silva, *Mind Control*.

Figure 7.1 The Mineral Element
The mineral world has a very fast inflow energy, marked by the arrows pointing inwards, and almost no outflow energy; that is the reason why most people call it dead. However, nothing is dead on this planet.

Figure 7.2 The Water Element
The water element still has a very fast inflow of energy but does give out some of this energy, especially the very fine etheric energy; the arrows indicate its energy exchange

The Element of Water

Undines live in every single moisture particle. There are millions, like the Gnomes, in an invisible space. Where is the limit on either side? Out there in space or in here in the minute particle?

The Element of Fire

The warmth of the fire element also causes light, but that light and warmth have perhaps lost the quality of love. This element now burns too hot and is often impure. It dazzles and hurts our eyes. The Salamander beings are tiny flecks of fire which are there to cleanse and illuminate. Because of the lack of human communica-

Figure 7.3 The Fire Element Fire Energy is a very special element. It is said that Prometheus stole it from the gods on Olympus and gave it to man against the wishes of the gods.

tion, the Salamanders have grown estranged and in their isolation cry out, often in anger saying, 'Hey, you, I am also here, take notice of me.'

Like neglected and ignored children, they often play naughty tricks until someone notices them. If they are kindly, lovingly approached they will, little by little, aid the human race again and shine brightly. They will no·longer burn but create warmth so that pure life can again evolve.

The Element of Air

With the element of air, the very breath of life, the duality of inhaling and exhaling in its rhythm was known to be the dance of the Sylphs. The human race has grossly misused this element by way of pollution, filling up the space of life where the ether could live, the Prana, the energy of spiritual angelic beings. Because of toxic gases, less and less constructive communication is being transmitted and the Sylphs, like all other elemental beings, now rebel. They even withdraw themselves and hide away. Human thanks for their service and human protection and blessing must return. We have to pour in love again; love because we wish to give it, and coming out of the absolute freedom to do so. Then communication will again be possible. Human souls who give to this element this new recognition will be found to return to health.

Figure 7.4 The Air Element The element of air, the breath of life has indeed its own breath. It breathes in to the time of two and out to the time of three. It is filled with etheric energy which is also known as prana

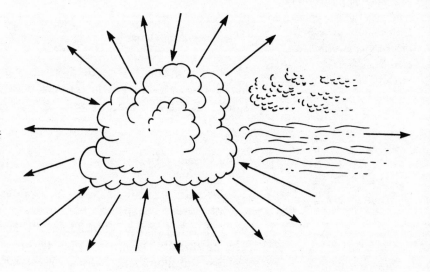

Likewise, in places where danger can cause death because of the lack of air, call upon the Sylphs with thanks, blessing and love, and help will be given to restore life because we have reunited ourselves with these creatures.

We should also link all of the elementals back to the angelic world and the great spiritual beings such as the Buddha, the Christ, Jehovah and Allah. This will enable them to speak to each other again. Man will then have learnt the languages of both these great kingdoms by speaking with the elementals and the angels and taking up the predestined place of the selfless and serving co-ordinator, the manager on behalf of the eternal Lord of Creation.

COMMUNICATION MEDITATIONS

1. *The mineral kingdom*

Relax and let go of all your daily concerns. Let the instrument, your body, go into calmness, peace and absolute harmony. With each exhalation, make sure that you are letting go of all tension.

Let the bright multi-colours in your busy mind disappear. Now wait for a deep blue to appear before your inner eye. Relax even more, allowing the golden light to dissolve all the petty pictures which you are still trying to hold before your mind. Think of a white, beautifully illuminated energy with a very fine, almost invisible magenta colour toned into this pure resurrected red. Red, the colour of the Father energy. The centre, the awareness, now turning into the energy of the son and daughter, the energy of love, a rose quartz colour.

Be thankful for this moment. Bless this time and love the communication which you are about to receive. Be open in safety. Your guide (the leader of such meditations) is aware that you are being protected. A guide in this context is an experienced master, tutor in charge; he/she must have enough consciousness so as to be aware at what stage anyone under his/her guidance has got to, otherwise the mind can go out of control and, again, mental illness can ensue.

You stand on the earth, a firm rock upon which we can depend for safety. We cannot be inside this rock as it is too dense, solid and hard. Yet, with our mind, we can slip into this dense, very compact space.

2.   *The water kingdom*

Relax and let go of all your daily concerns. Let the instrument, your body, go into calmness, peace and absolute harmony. With each exhalation, make sure that you are letting go of all tension.

Let the bright multi-colours in your busy mind disappear. Now wait for a deep blue to appear before your inner eye. Relax even more, allowing the golden light to dissolve all the petty pictures which you are still trying to hold before your mind. Think of a white, beautifully illuminated energy with a very fine, almost invisible magenta colour toned into this pure resurrected red. Red, the colour of the Father energy. The centre, the awareness, now turning into the energy of the son and daughter, the energy of love, a rose quartz colour.

Be thankful for this moment. Bless this time and love the communication which you are about to receive. Be open in safety. Your guide (the leader of such meditations) is aware that you are being protected.

Water. The water of life. The chalice filled from the fountain where water is carrying the life, the reflected light and the caressing love.

Water is the home of the Undines. These water elementals are the carriers of etheric living energy which once came down from the great cosmic ether and has anchored itself in water, to heal, to cleanse, to refresh body, soul and spirit.

The Undine kingdom is present in the energies in the warm state when fire (Salamanders) play with the Undines and create in their play a warm, life-enhancing moisture which we can breathe in, healing our bodies with an enhanced breath of life. See this chalice lifted up to your lips. Take into your senses its scent, its fragrance. The two energies of water Undines and fire Salamanders create the third energy of living fragrance. As they dance, they create the new forms and new forms give new life. See on the floor where they have been, the traces left. These are like seeds lying in the fertile earth. The Gnomes are taking care of them. We stand high up and look down on to this wonderful dance floor. As we look, we can see that the seeds all sprout and, behold, what wonderful patterns are now visible.

In a creative way we wonder. As we wonder, we are already creating new ideas on how to follow the dance, to learn the new dance. We now thank the Undines for their inspiration. Out of the silence we hear a sound, a singing. The music of the Undines mingles with the music of the angels, the music of the spheres. The singing sound changes into harmonies hitherto not heard by us. This is a direct result of our humble effort to communicate as best we know how.

We are learning, we are beginning to interpret our own, however incomplete, speech with both the elementals and the angels.

We are now using the circle of light and the cross of light in the circle of light as a golden key to close the centres of higher perception securely. The crown, the brow, the throat, the heart, the solar plexus, the sacral and the base energy centre.

Remember where you started the meditation, the room, the house, and when you are ready you may open your eyes and be fully returned.

Amen (or) So be it.

3.   *The fire kingdom*

Relax and let go of all your daily concerns. Let the instrument, your body, go into calmness, peace and absolute harmony. With each exhalation, make sure that you are letting go of all tension.

Let the bright multi-colours in your busy mind disappear. Now wait for a deep blue to appear before your inner eye. Relax even more, allowing the golden light to dissolve all the petty pictures which you are still trying to hold before your mind. Think of a white, beautifully illuminated energy with a very fine, almost invisible magenta colour toned into this pure resurrected red. Red the colour of the Father energy. The centre, the awareness, now turning into the energy of the son and daughter, the energy of love, a rose quartz colour.

Be thankful for this moment. Bless this time and love the communication which you are about to receive. Be open in safety. Your guide (the leader of such meditations) is aware that you are being protected.

Try and see it like a cube, a space which is like a tiny room with four walls, a floor and a ceiling all of the same size. Look inside, imagining it to be on the palm of your hand. You see thousands of even smaller cubes inside this tiny room. In each there are uncountable little Gnomes, all busy creating and maintaining this mineral substance.

Now, it has become alive in your mind's eye. It is no longer just matter, it is living matter which is at all times ready to serve you. It will serve you even more if you think how it needs your thanks for being, just being. It can change when you bless it and love it. The Gnomes will then be at your command and prevent any mishaps. You can tell them to make this matter strong, to hold it together in the way that you wish it to be, so that it can serve you. Now you have to be aware of the reason for this. Why do you need this matter which has been built to serve you? Are you using it for the service of others or is it being used for your own selfish gain? Examine your motives. You can only truly be thankful for this matter, shaped for your use, if it is used in a way which can help those who are as yet not as awake as you are.

To be awake means to know and to employ the knowledge in such a way that it serves those whom you meet.

Now you can bless it and the Gnomes can become aware of your gift. To them this blessing is similar to your daily bread. Then send to them love, because you know that in the end this is the most precious gift that you can offer.

In the peace and stillness you can now communicate. Be silent for a while. Listen, let go of any thoughts, just listen, listen with your other, inner ears. At present we have lost this capacity and it will take some time before we again reach this level of hearing. Try to listen, really listen. When we learn a new language, it takes some time to really know it. We first have to learn, to understand the actual speaking. This is always very difficult. Have patience.

Now turn your inner gaze to the vast spaces outside of the tiny room which you hold in your hand. Think how you could tell the angels what you have experienced. Again, to begin with, you cannot form any words as these are of the earth. Just look, and you will with your inner eyes begin to see. Allow all the conventional pictures of angels to go away, to dissolve into a vast open room, a hall where the walls, ceiling and floor are too far away to see. A very small part of the great angelic being is there. The whole of this inconceivable great being we cannot as yet comprehend. A great sound of deepest singing, ringing, fills the hall. There is no time or space. You are alone, but not lonely. No one else is here, but all are here. There is a fulfilled energy and we can only add wonder, awe and reverence. Can we take the thanks, the blessings and the love which we communicated to the Gnomes and lay it into this enormous place? Yes, we can.

The singing sound changes into harmonies hitherto not heard by us. This is a direct result of our humble effort to communicate as best we know how. (See *The Book of Sound Therapy* by Olivia Dewhurst-Maddock.)

We are learning, we are beginning to interpret our own, however incomplete, speaking, with both the elementals and the angels.

We are now using the circle of light and the cross of light in the circle of light as a golden key to close the centres of higher perception securely. The crown, the brow, the throat, the heart, the solar plexus, the sacral and the base energy centre.

Remember where you started the meditation, the room, the house, and when you are ready, you may open your eyes and be fully returned.

Amen (or) So be it.

Note

In this meditation and the following ones the student in meditation training will be shown graphically the circle of light and the cross of light in the circle of light.

1. The circle is the symbol of surrounding in a protective way; in this case the circle is the colour of gold.
2. The cross is the reminder of being conscious and is almost white with some rose quartz colour in it.
3. The complete symbol is then visualized over each chakra as the meditation closes.

This is vital to bring the student back into the here-and-now world after meditation.

Light and warmth are around us. The inner light and the inner warmth. When we need the help of the Salamanders they can turn cold into warmth and can turn darkness into light.

We are inside a cave; there is at present no light and it is very cold. Relax, let go of any tension. Trust that you are protected and that no harm will come to you.

A tiny spark of light in the distance begins to flicker. It is coming nearer and starts to be a stable, fine light. It now comes closer to us, and little by little, very peacefully burns brighter. The Salamander beings are basically very shy and like to make sure that they are welcome. Indeed, they respond to love which comes from the hearts of human beings and protects them. They are also shy towards the elemental beings of water, the Undines, and also shy away from the Sylphs, the elementals of the air. If both of these elementals are very gentle towards the Salamanders, they can play together and create surprising effects.

Now the Salamander beings are before you in uncountable numbers. They spread a beautiful light all over the cave. With this light also comes a gentle warmth. Now the cave is a most wonderful place. It reveals itself to be like the hall in a very special palace. Everything shines in a golden colour. The gold of wisdom. Because we have offered love, the response is all around us. We seem to be in the centre of a universal heart which reflects the love we offered and has created this most precious palace for us. All is built out of warmth and light, gentle light, loving warmth.

We say 'thank-you' for this beautiful experience, we bless the moment of our vision and we leave forever our love for the Salamanders.

The singing sound changes into harmonies hitherto not heard by us. This is a direct result of our humble effort to communicate as best we know how.

We are learning, we are beginning to interpret our own, however incomplete, speech with both the elementals and the angels.

We are now using the circle of light and the cross of light in the circle of light as a golden key to close the centres of higher perception securely. The crown, the brow, the throat, the heart, the solar plexus, the sacral and the base energy centre.

Remember where you started the meditation, the room, the house and when you are ready, you may open your eyes and be fully returned.

Amen (or) So be it

4.   *The air kingdom*

Relax and let go of all your daily concerns. Let the instrument, your body, go into calmness, peace and absolute harmony. With each exhalation make sure that you are letting go of all tension.

Let the bright multi-colours in your busy mind disappear. Now wait for a deep blue to appear before your inner eye. Relax even more, allowing the golden light to dissolve all the petty pictures which you are still trying to hold before your mind. Think of a white, beautifully illuminated energy with a fine, almost invisible magenta colour toned into this pure resurrected red. Red, the colour of the Father energy. The centre, the awareness, now turning into the energy of the son and daughter, the energy of love, a rose quartz colour.

Be thankful for this moment. Bless this time and love the communication which you are about to receive. Be open in safety. Your guide (the leader of such meditations) is aware that you are being protected.

A beautiful garden lies before you and you enter this garden by walking across the meadow. Countless flowers are close to your feet. Shrubs and trees are on either side of you. Stand still, wait and look more closely and absorb what you are seeing surrounding you. As you stand there, it is important that you feel no wish to hurry. You sit down on the soft grass. Peace and relaxation overcome you and a beautiful blue light dawns inside your third eye. This light spreads all over you, enabling you to relax completely into the environment. The blue slowly changes into a calm gold light. It makes the space that you are in appear larger. A very gentle breeze moves your hair, caresses your skin and you become aware that your breath is very slow and very deep. What is this air that you are using in order to live? If it keeps you alive, it in itself must be alive. You ask, 'What are you, air?' Out of this stillness comes a whisper:

'I was part of God. I am all around you. As you need me, so I need you. We are intertwined. You are able to change me because I can only partly help you. The other part of me which you cannot use is the part used by the trees, shrubs and flowers. You can help to reunite me with the wholeness which I once was.'

'What is it that I can do for you? Have you got a name?'

'Yes, I do have a name, but firstly, I am not able to be a single being. I am actually we, so you talk to all of us.'

'Please tell me then what you call yourselves, all of you.'

'We are known as the Sylphs, the elemental spirits of the air.'

'How can I be of help to you?'

'Take us back to the great energy of God and the angels. You can talk to the angels but we can no longer do this. You humans have come between us and the original wholeness of us. Talk to the angels and tell them about our state now.'

'How have you changed? Why are you saying this about your state now?'

'You took the first step to freedom, to become separate from God when you took the fruit from the Tree of Knowledge. You now know the secrets of God, but you have forgotten the life, the

Tree of Life. The breath of air is no longer the same since you used your knowledge. The air which we are now is heavy with wrongly used knowledge. You cannot change this back to the living state unless you change a part of yourself. You humans have forgotten in all your great knowledge that gratitude, blessing and love are all part of the purity of life. The living breath of air needs to be regained. When you come to us with the three great gifts of love, thanks and blessing, we will help you to achieve this task.

Tell the trees and the plants that you will give to them the part of the air, the part of us, which you are unable to use. If you become a mediator between us and the angels, you will be a creator of a new air, a new breath of life. This new air and breath of life will start a new cycle because you have changed us. Unless you help us, all the air must die, also us and you. Must we all die? No. If you can follow the path of love, blessing and gratitude, we will all have created a new and very beautiful breath of love, much more alive than it was at the beginning.'

'Can I see you Sylphs?'

'Yes you can if you can deeply relax. Relax, and now, what can you see?'

'Is what I see correct? Are you completely invisible, transparent beings. Uncountable numbers of you in the tiniest space?'

'So you can see us.'

'Yes, I think I can.'

'Yes, you have now seen us. We dance around and within you. We also dance around and within all plants. But, it is only you that can make the new air. Only you who can redeem us out of the present state where we are captive in this heavy air. Change yourself, and you will change the universe for all eternity to come.'

We must have sat here for a long time talking to the sylphs. We now need to go about our daily work knowing that the changes which we have to make we will work with each day. We will thank, we will bless, we will love the sylphs and we will also talk to the angels about them.

Now you have found the little garden where you can communicate with the sylphs and the angels. You are now taking up your task and you go into the world of substance where you count, weigh and measure, but now you add the new ingredient of thanks, blessing and love.

The singing sound changes into harmonies hitherto not heard by us. This is a direct result of our humble effort to communicate as best we know how.

We are learning, we are beginning to interpret our own, how-ever incomplete, speaking with both the elementals and the angels.

We are now using the circle of light and the cross of light in the circle of light as a golden key to close the centres of higher perception securely. The crown, the brow, the throat, the heart, the solar plexus, the sacral and the base energy centre.

Remember where you started the meditation, the room, the house and when you are ready you may open your eyes and be fully returned.

Amen (or) So be it

5.   *The etheric energy of life*

Relax and let go of all your daily concerns. Let the instrument, your body, go into calmness, peace and absolute harmony. With each exhalation, make sure that you are letting go of all tension.

Let the bright multi-colours in your busy mind disappear. Now wait for a deep blue to appear before your inner eye. Relax even more, allowing the golden light to dissolve all the petty pictures which you are still trying to hold before your mind. Think of a white, beautifully illuminated energy with a very fine, almost invisible magenta colour toned into this pure resurrected red. Red, the colour of the Father energy. The centre, the awareness, now turning into the energy of the son and daughter, the energy of love, a rose quartz colour.

Be thankful for this moment. Bless this time and love the communication which you are about to receive. Be open in safety. Your guide (the leader of such meditations), is aware that you are being protected.

We are going into the night, out into the vast space which is without borders, but we have decided that we are very safe. There are beautiful 'wings' of protection around us.

The darkness is not really dark but it has the colour of a deep indigo-violet; it is warm, it is full of beauty. Sparkling around us are gold stars which make such wonderful patterns that we cannot yet find any repeats or pictures that we recognize.

We become aware of a presence of energy that seems to have the form of very fine and noble features. Through this wonderful deep colour of the indigo-violet shines an image created out of light. Not a strong light, not a blinding light but a gentle and yet

Figure 7.5 The Chalice

```
1 BEHIND
2 BELOW
3 LEFT
4 RIGHT
5 FRONT
6 ABOVE
7 WITHIN
    8 DARKNESS
        9 LIGHT
            10 COLOUR
                11 SOUND
                    12 FORM
13 THE ONE, CONTAINING
   TIME AND SPACE
```

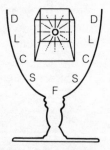

The symbolic meaning of the cup, the chalice, goes back to all ancient rites and in most of these rites it stands for the fullness of life, and indeed, includes the spirit and life force from the world of the divine, grace and the invisible energy of God.

very clear light that makes out the features of a most elevated being. We recognize in it the perfect image of a spiritual being who is eternally young and yet beautifully mature. We are drawn to it to be united with it. We sense that it is part of us and yet a being of energy which is far more alive than we are. Part of this life we recognize within us and it is like a mirror which reflects the perfect life force which we also have within us.

It is as if we were seeing now an unending ocean of life force which breathes like waves in and out with a rhythm of eternity. The gold, the light, the deep indigo-violet is reflected in it and has this eternal everlasting beauty. As we now look down at our own feet, standing very close to this ocean, we can see our own image and we can see that we seem to bear a very close likeness to this great being as if we were just only one cell of it but in its existence is again the whole. We are asked to accept from this eternal energy a part so that we become a part of this great wholeness. We seem to drink, as though it were out of a chalice, the energy which is now all around us. As we accept this wonderfully refreshing, renewing, reviving, rejuvenating drink, we begin to see ourselves as part of this life force which is eternal.

We look up and see once more the immensely wonderful image and hands which seem to offer this to us, which stretch out towards us and we accept in gratitude this gift. It says to us: take this, close it into your heart and guard it so that life never ebbs for you. Accept, transform and release so that you are a pure channel of communication between the angels and the elemental beings. You can become an eternally well, flowing being like we are.

Remember that you are returning now to the place where you have 'left' your body and visualize the room or space where you started your meditation.

We are now using the circle of light and the cross of light in the circle of light as a golden key to close the centres of higher perception securely. The crown, the brow, the throat, the heart, the solar plexus, the sacral and the base energy centre.

In Figure 7.5, protection is from all sides, below and above, finally centring the person within. This becomes 'the space'.

Time development follows from unknown darkness to an awareness of its opposite – light. Then gradual slowing down creates the colours, the sounds and lastly, the most permanent stage, matter, (which indeed is not permanent seen in the perspective of life) which is the form element, frozen music.

Then both space and time are surrounded by one energy, making a dedication of thirteen steps.

Conclusion

We have examined colour from many points of view: science, which measures, weighs and counts; the spiritual path which can only be appreciated through the human heart; and the heart which knows the truth and can tell if things are real or unreal, without needing any scientific proof. You and I have experienced colour and all its energies, through all the phenomena and through the power of visualization.

Life is eternal in spite of all the appraisals and logical conclusions; but through the imagination that leads to art and beauty, life appears in stages which are immeasurable. Life was, is, and will be immeasurable for ever; that's why it is alive.

The art is to translate the information we receive into the words of language. Perfect art can be like poetry which does not allow only logic to rule, but when words are united with other words, they can suddenly change their meaning:

> CUTHMAN: This is the morning to take the air, flute-clear
> And, like a lutanist, with a hand of wind
> Playing the responsive hills, till a long vibration
> Spills across the fields, and the chancelled larches
> Sing like Lenten choirboys, a green treble;
> Playing at last the skylark into rising,
> The wintered cuckoo to a bashful stutter.
> It is the first day of the year that I've king'd
> Myself on the rock, sat myself in the wind:
> It was laying my face on gold.
>
> Christopher Fry, *The Boy with a Cart*

Could you also try this using unusual colours and see what they say to each other?

I have tried to convey in the chapters of this book, ideas, reality, art, psychic experiences and visualizations which appeal to both the brain and the heart of man.

Colour is a living medium, so sensitive that it is actually affected by the slightest alterations and degrees of light. You may have come across some thoughts expressed in this book which you cannot take on board. You must, however, allow logic, reason and material reality to mix or communicate with feeling, sensitivity and love. When you do this you will never stop growing.

At first all things seem to be overwhelming and so complex that you cannot see the wood for the trees. But then you realize that you are in the wood and that each tree has an individual self to add to the wood. When this is happening, then you can relax and accept this complexity. Suddenly all becomes far more simple and you will see that love embraces all and logic divides all. Both need each other to find a way, a way which we all tread, thinking we are all alone. One day we suddenly arrive in a clearing and find all the others, who also thought that they were lost, alone and full of fear and then we suddenly recognize each other.

So it is that all the colours make up the rainbow, they remain recognized as each individual colour but also as the rainbow.

Finally, each colour is a family of beings within which each individual has the particular hue to make the colour real. Is it not strange that colour has had to go so long unrecognized as a reality among all the vibrations which are used in science?

Its beauty has, perhaps, blinded so many because it has been the medium which makes this world such a 'garden'. Yet this beautiful colourful garden is vital in our healing.

The true meaning and importance of colour are gradually being recognized and it is as if it is about to be crowned as the supreme being through which is projected to mankind life, beauty, energy and harmonization.

Perhaps it is the step we finally have to take when so much has not really worked, and when it finally becomes recognized that it needs to be used in the world of healing, it will become the means by which humans can absorb in the most gentle way, the vibrations that colours have, which carry life and health back into the discordant structures of modern lifestyles, where so little is beautiful and everything must be practical and useful. Colour combined with other harmonies, such as music and beautiful forms, will bring together the complete spectrum.

GLOSSARY

Aniline   A chemical dye, very poisonous.

Asthma   A condition connected to breathing difficulties. Can occur as a result of shocks, either mental, emotional or physical.

Autism   A mental condition which can cause schizophrenia.

Ayurveda   The original Indian medical practice using colour and gem stones.

Babbitt, Edwin, D.   (1828–1905). Studied in depth the electro-magnetic spectrum and its use in healing, and linked light and colour to universal energies and the divinity of man. See Bibliography.

Beesley, Ronald   (1905–1979). A colour healer with the gift of clairvoyance. See Bibliography.

Besant, Annie   (1847–1933). Member of the Theosophical Society. Studied the Tibetan sacred wisdom and order of the human being.

Byzantine   A culture that was very prominent at the time of Pythagoras right into the fifth century AD. Originally the city of Constantinople. Its influence stretched into the North Italian cities of Ravenna and Venice with the beautiful colours used in their mosaic art. It always had strong connections with Greece.

Camphill Schools   Educational establishments for the care of mentally handicapped children and adults.

Chagall, Marc   (1887–1949). Born in Russia and studied in Paris. Artist and designer of church windows. For example, the Stephans Kirche in Mainz, Germany, his last major work.

Chakra   A Sanskrit word meaning 'wheel'. These are thought to have some connection with endocrine glands in the human body.

Claustrophobia   A condition, mainly mental, of being unable to endure small spaces or being in a crowd. Agoraphobia, the complementary problem, involves being unable to stand too much space without the security of an enclosed room.

Dinshah, P. Ghadiali   (1873–1966). Came from Malaga, New Jersey, USA, and held many honorary degrees. His colour therapy claimed much success. Further information can be obtained from the Spectrachrome Institute, Malaga, New Jersey. See Bibliography.

Dowsing Very precise information about this work is available from The Society of Dowsers.

The Egyptian Book of the Dead It is known that the title has been wrongly translated and the symbols could also have meant 'The Egyptian Book of the Living'. It is actually a kind of instruction book, like the Old Testament or the Koran.

Electro-magnetic spectrum The measurement of all the vibrations as far as can be scientifically established. This includes very high cosmic rays (vibrations too fast for physical measurement), down to very slow sound waves (7–14 cycles per second) when these low frequencies can actually destroy all biochemical structures.

Electronic ballast In layman's terms, a converter which changes AC into DC, causing the electricity to become constant. It is used for fluorescent lights, stabilizing the gas used in the tubes and cutting out all flicker.

Fibonacci, Leonardo (1175–1250). A Florentine mathematician who described the Fibonacci sequence of numbers. A contemporary of Francis of Assisi.

Fluorescent A term used to describe the illumination issued by the gas-filled tubes which H. Heitler developed. The luminosity produced in certain substances also connected to X-rays and ultra-violet rays. See also *Ott, John*.

Francis, St (1182–1226). A monk who lived in Assisi. The founder of the Franciscan order. He is probably among the most well-known saints of the Christian faith.

Galvanizer, skin The use of a sensitive instrument which records the tension of a person under certain environmental influences.

Geode Stones with hollow cavities studded interiorly with crystals such as amethysts, quartz crystals and many other precious or semi-precious stones. Inside, quite frequently, is also found the still-liquid form of the growing crystals which obeys the laws of the geological crystallization of certain substances.

Glazewski, Dr Father Andrew (1901–73). A concert pianist and doctor of physics, he worked for nine years in the Vatican. He was also a great healer and studied Rudolf Steiner and anthroposophy.

Goethe, Johann Wolfgang von (1749–1832). Scientist, poet and researcher, born in Frankfurt. See Bibliography.

Goetheanum The school founded by Rudolf Steiner in 1911 in Dornach, Switzerland, to teach anthroposophy, a science to study man as part of the spiritual energies which stand behind all visible structures.

Gregory, Ronald Professor of Psychology at Bristol University.

Gurdjieff, G. Russian mystic. See Ouspensky (Bibliography).

Heitler, Dr Hans (1899–1979). Physicist, expelled from Germany as a Jew. Worked under Professor Powell, Bristol University, in outer space research. Developed the first fluorescent tubes emergency illuminations.

Incandescent   The normal light bulbs which have a metallic filament which absorbs about 70% of electricity producing heat, and about 30% light.

König, Dr Karl   (1902–1966). Founder of the Campbell and Sheiling schools. Author and researcher.

Mantra   A sacred word or prayer which has the power to bring about physical and spiritual change when used as directed by a teacher or master.

Monochrome   Any item or object having only one colour of even hue.

The New Testament   A book containing the synoptic gospels and other teachings. It is known that other gospels existed which have not been published.

Newton, Sir Isaac   (1642–1727). Early English scientist who researched the natural phenomena of colour, gravity and their relationship to consciousness. See Bibliography.

The Old Testament   This book belongs to the teachings of the Jewish and Christian faiths. To some extent it is also part of the sacred teachings for the Moslems. All religions have their writings on human conduct and how to 'see' God. Through translations and the changes in human consciousness, many passages have often been left out or not really understood.

Osiris   Egyptian god of the sun.

Ott, Dr John   Member of the Light and Health Research Council (MLHRC). The originator of the full spectrum fluorescent tube. Researcher into children's learning capacity and into illumination. His contribution to interior illumination is world-famous and very important.

Psyche   The Greek word for the human soul.

Spine   The divisions which constitute the spine are as follows: skull, cervical, thoracic, lumbar, sacrum and coccyx.

Steiner, Dr Rudolf   (1861–1925). Founder of the Anthroposophical Society, Dornach, Switzerland. He developed a spiritual science of the origin, make-up and function of the human. Not a religious order.

Thoth   The Egyptian god of writing, sciences and inventor of the arts, who kept a record of the actions of the dead.

BIBLIOGRAPHY

Alpen, Dr Frank, *Exploring Atlantis*, Arizona Metaphysical Society, 1981.

Babbitt, Edwin D., *The Principles of Light and Colour*, 1878.

Beesley, Ronald, *The Robe of Many Colours*, private publication, 1968.

Beesley, Ronald, *The Creative Ether*, Neville Spearman, 1972.

Cade, Maxwell, *The Awakened Mind*, Element Books, 1989.

Critchlow, Keith, *Order in Space*, Thames & Hudson, 1969.

Dewhurst-Maddock, Olivia, *The Book of Sound Therapy*, Gaia, 1993.

Dinshah, P. Ghadiali, *Spectrochrome Metry Encyclopaedia*, 3 vols., 1939.

Garde, Dr R.K., *Ayurveda for Health and Long Life*, D.B. Taraporevala Sons & Co. Private Ltd, India, 1975.

Gimbel, Theophilus, *Healing through Colour*, C.W. Daniel, 1980.

Gimbel, Theophilus, *Form, Sound, Colour and Healing*, C.W. Daniel, 1987.

Goethe, Johann Wolfgang von, *Die Farben Lehre* (The Teachings of Colour), 1810.

Haich, Elisabeth, *Initiation*, Mandala, 1979.

Hunt, Roland, *The Seven Keys to Colour Healing*, 11th edn, C.W. Daniel.

Kilian, J., *Crystals, Secrets of the Inorganic*, Scientific Book Club, 1940.

Kilner, Dr Walter John, *The Human Atmosphere* (orig. title, republished as *The Aura*), 1911.

Lüscher, Professor Max, *The Lüscher Colour Test*, Cape, 1969.

New Larousse Encyclopaedia of Mythology, Hamlyn, 1959.

Newton, Sir Isaac, *Philosophiae Naturalis Principia Mathematica*, 1687.

Ouseley, S.G.J., *The Power of the Rays*, L.N. Fowler, 1951.

Ouspensky, P.D., *In Search of the Miraculous*, Routledge Kegan Paul, 1949.

Pearl, Richard H., *Introduction to the Mineral Kingdom*, Blandford Press, London, 1966.

Prouskauer, Herrman, O., *Zum Studium von Goethes Farbenlehre*, Zbinden Verlag, Basel, 1968.

Silva, José, *Mind Control*.

Thakkur, Dr Chandra Shekhar, G., *Ayurveda: The Science of Life*, ASI Publishers Inc., New York, 1974.

Tisserand, Robert B., *The Art of Aroma Therapy*, C.W. Daniel, 1977.

Watson, Lyall, *Supernature*, Hodder & Stoughton, London, 1973.
Wills, Pauline, *The Reflexology and Colour Therapy Workbook*, Element, 1992.
–, *Health Essentials: Colour Therapy*, Element, 1993.

Index